D0400093

"We all need to sell ourselves and this b\ guide on how to do that. This book is full of useful career advice – and brought to life by fascinating examples and often surprising insights."

Rhymer Rigby, writer for *The Telegraph* and *Financial Times* and author of *28 Business Thinkers Who Changed the World*

"*How to Stand Out* covers the latest evidence on body language, communication and persuasion. It's a rigorously researched, compelling and sometimes surprising read no matter what your goals in life. You will undoubtedly learn something new."

Dr Tomas Chamorro-Premuzic, CEO of Hogan Assessments, and Professor of Business Psychology at University College London and Columbia University

"Engaging, no-nonsense and full of scientifically proven advice – an essential book for anyone wanting to outshine the crowd and get ahead in business and life."

Dr. Michael Sinclair, co-author of *Mindfulness for Busy People*, Founder & Clinical Director, City Psychology Group

"An easy read with some well researched, practical and evidence-backed advice. Definitely stands out from the crowd and can easily be applied straight away."

Paul Hughes, Executive Development Director at Cranfield School of Management

"An extraordinary book for everybody: Dr Yeung's book presents a wealth of useful tips on how to build your confidence and stand out from the crowd. This book is a treasure trove of useful tips on how to outperform in a job interview, get promoted, win more customers, get your business funded or simply become more successful in life."

Professor Khalid Hafeez, Dean of The Claude Littner Business School at the University of West London

"Practical, accessible tips and techniques for making yourself more interesting to clients, customers, and friends!"

Tamara Box, Partner and Global Chair of the Financial Industry Group at international law firm Reed Smith LLP

"Once again, Rob Yeung demonstrates how challenge can quickly become opportunity. He has the uncanny knack of identifying our insecurities, helping us view them from a different angle and transforming them into foundation stones for building new confidence. Whether you want to learn to 'talk like TED', present your best side at a job interview, or simply want to stand out from the crowd – this new book offers simple, clear and practical guidance. Like his previous books, this is another example of why Dr Rob Yeung stands out from other psychologists and coaches."

Malcolm Green, Creative Chairman at advertising agency Green Cave People

How To Stand Out

Proven Tactics for Getting Noticed

Dr Rob Yeung

CAPSTONE
A Wiley Brand

This edition first published 2015

© 2015 Dr Rob Yeung

Registered office
John Wiley and Sons Ltd, The Atrium, Southern Gate, Chichester, West Sussex, PO19 8SQ, United Kingdom

For details of our global editorial offices, for customer services and for information about how to apply for permission to reuse the copyright material in this book please see our website at www.wiley.com.

The right of the author to be identified as the author of this work has been asserted in accordance with the Copyright, Designs and Patents Act 1988.

All rights reserved. No part of this publication may be reproduced, stored in a retrieval system, or transmitted, in any form or by any means, electronic, mechanical, photocopying, recording or otherwise, except as permitted by the UK Copyright, Designs and Patents Act 1988, without the prior permission of the publisher.

Wiley publishes in a variety of print and electronic formats and by print-on-demand. Some material included with standard print versions of this book may not be included in e-books or in print-on-demand. If this book refers to media such as a CD or DVD that is not included in the version you purchased, you may download this material at http://booksupport.wiley.com. For more information about Wiley products, visit www.wiley.com.

Designations used by companies to distinguish their products are often claimed as trademarks. All brand names and product names used in this book and on its cover are trade names, service marks, trademark or registered trademarks of their respective owners. The publisher and the book are not associated with any product or vendor mentioned in this book. None of the companies referenced within the book have endorsed the book.

Limit of Liability/Disclaimer of Warranty: While the publisher and author have used their best efforts in preparing this book, they make no representations or warranties with the respect to the accuracy or completeness of the contents of this book and specifically disclaim any implied warranties of merchantability or fitness for a particular purpose. It is sold on the understanding that the publisher is not engaged in rendering professional services and neither the publisher nor the author shall be liable for damages arising herefrom. If professional advice or other expert assistance is required, the services of a competent professional should be sought.

Library of Congress Cataloging-in-Publication Data

Yeung, Rob, 1971–
  How to stand out : proven tactics for getting noticed / Dr. Rob Yeung.
    pages cm
  Includes index.
  ISBN 978-0-85708-425-5 (paperback)
  1. Success in business. 2. Self-confidence. I. Title.
  HF5386.Y4798 2015
  650.1—dc23

                                                    2015021595

A catalogue record for this book is available from the British Library.

ISBN 978-0-857-08425-5 (pbk)
ISBN 978-0-857-08423-1 (ebk)   ISBN 978-0-857-08422-4 (ebk)

Cover design: Wiley

Set in 10/13 pt SabonLTStd by Aptara
Printed in Great Britain by TJ International Ltd, Padstow, Cornwall, UK

Contents

About the Author

Dr Rob Yeung is an organizational psychologist at consultancy Talentspace, where he runs leadership development programmes for executives as well as training workshops on topics such as presentation skills, confidence, teamwork and personal productivity. He also coaches individuals and lectures to university and business school students.

In addition, he is an in-demand keynote speaker at conferences worldwide. He is frequently asked to speak on topics such as the psychology of leadership, sales success, change and high achievement. In both his consulting work and keynote speeches, he distinguishes himself by basing his recommendations on scientific research.

He is the author of over 20 books, including the bestsellers *How To Win: The Argument, the Pitch, the Job, the Race* (Capstone) and *E is for Exceptional: The New Science of Success* (Pan Books).

www.robyeung.com

www.twitter.com/robyeung

www.facebook.com/drrobyeung

Acknowledgements

Thanks must go first and foremost to the scores of clients, entrepreneurs, leaders and other standout individuals who took the time out of their busy lives to talk to me. I'm sorry that not all of your stories made it into the book but my editors were brutal about the page count! You have my undying gratitude and I know that readers will grasp and enjoy the principles within this book so much more by hearing your stories, understanding your struggles and triumphs, and discovering what you learnt.

Thank you to the Capstone team headed by Holly Bennion too. I appreciate that you want me to write the best book I can. Your support and candid, yet gently put, criticisms hopefully make my book all the better for readers.

Thank you Steve Cuthbertson too. You more than anyone else have to put up with the up and down rollercoaster of my emotions. Your quiet resilience is like a force field that helps to keep the outside world at bay. Without it, I don't know how I would ever get much done.

And final thanks must go to my parents: Stephen and Judy. You have always supported and encouraged me. You have allowed me to craft my own life and career for as long as I can remember. For this and so much else, you will always have my thanks and love.

Introduction

When you do the common things in life in an uncommon
way, you will command the attention of the world.

George Washington Carver

What is it that helps some people stand out? What helps
certain individuals get picked out of the crowd – to
attract attention and get noticed at work, at a party, in
life?

I'm not talking about metaphorical crowds either. How do people
stand out when they are in a literal crowd, say a room full of people
at a networking event all clamouring for attention?

These were the kinds of questions I was looking to answer when I
went to a networking breakfast one sunny but unexpectedly cold
spring morning in west London. The venue: Lala Brasserie, a glass-
fronted Mediterranean restaurant by a busy intersection. I'd been
told by one of the organizers that the regular meeting began at
6.45 a.m. However, when I turned up exactly on time, I was confronted by the bustle and noise of a room thronged with scores of
people already deep in conversation. It turned out that, such was the
desire to get talking and do deals, most people turned up at 6.30 a.m.
Being almost one of the last to arrive, I had some catching up to do.

In quick succession, I met one person after the next. Marvin ran a
company offering bookkeeping services. Zane was an employment

1

lawyer. Serena, a designer of bespoke jewellery. There was Anastacia, who worked in foreign exchange. Thayne, an electrician. I met so many people that the names and faces began to blur.

At around 7.15 a.m. came the opportunity for everyone to address the whole room. The chairperson of the meeting – a strong-featured Irish woman with her hair pulled away from her face in a business-like manner – called for our attention. In a strident voice, she invited us to tell the room individually what we did and what we were looking for. It was our opportunity to pitch ourselves.

To keep the introductions moving swiftly, someone at the back of the room must have been sitting with a timer. A bell rang every 50 seconds – not even a full minute! – to keep people from hogging airtime.

There was a financial adviser, a landscape gardener, a virtual personal assistant, the owner of a firm of commercial cleaners. Graphic and Web designers, a guy who did something with email, a physiotherapist, a commercial property expert.

Twenty people had spoken but that wasn't even half of the people in the room. I was trying my best to pay attention but most of it simply wasn't sticking. Was Jacinta the therapist or was she something to do with charities? Who was the tall guy with curly grey hair and the glasses again? Yet still they came. More: an architect, several different kinds of lawyer, a telemarketer and a self-described "business growth engineer". For the most part, I couldn't keep track.

Many spoke too quietly to be heard in front of the 50-strong audience. A few read from scraps of paper in monotone voices without looking at the increasingly bored faces around them. Yet a few stood out.

A man with a lined face and a gravelly but sincere voice called Merik started with what the audience immediately realized were lyrics from a song: "I believe the children are our future. Teach them

2

well and let them lead the way." He paused dramatically and then said, "You know the rest."

And of course we did. By quoting the opening lines to the well-known Whitney Houston song *The Greatest Love*, he had struck a chord with most of us and made himself instantly memorable.

He went on to say that he believed that children are the future. And that children in schools needed clean windows to be able to see properly, concentrate properly, study properly. So he asked if anyone knew of any schools that needed their windows cleaning. It was a quirky, unusual pitch for his commercial window cleaning business. And for that reason it stood out like a lighthouse on a foggy night.

Another of the small handful that stood out: Luke, a ballsy estate agent in his twenties – he looked and sounded like he could play the cheeky-but-lovable rogue on any British soap opera. He told the room how he had valued the houses of a couple of older women recently. He estimated that they could sell their houses for in excess of £1.2 million. But they had bought their houses years and years ago for around £8,000. The implication: on selling up, these women would become instant cash millionaires.

Luke joked that he didn't know if his insurance covered him should he give an elderly lady a heart attack and the throng laughed warmly for perhaps the first time that morning. Again, he managed to distinguish himself from the crowd.

The science of standing out

Think about some of the people you know who stand out. What is it that helps them get noticed? Is it that they speak slowly and forcefully – or perhaps quickly and with acerbic humour? Do they listen and make others feel like the centre of the universe? Or do they just radiate some kind of charm and good humour that draws others to them?

We're talking about star quality here. The reasons why one individual gets promoted again and again while others languish behind. The reasons why certain salespeople or small-business owners win new customers or clients seemingly without effort. The reasons why one person gets asked on date after date while others struggle to meet the right person.

How To Stand Out is for anyone who wants to make an impact, to get noticed for professional or personal reasons. This book is for you if you're a business owner hungry to sell more products and services – or maybe a freelance worker who needs to sell yourself. Perhaps you're a fundraiser or campaigner who needs to get your directives across more robustly, a scientist seeking to communicate your findings or a policymaker seeking to change your community. Or you yearn to socialize more easily or even find love. Through word and deed, this book will help you to be more engaging, entertaining and persuasive. It will help you to *stand out.*

This book will help you to be more engaging, entertaining and persuasive.

Finding techniques that work

So why do *I* want to write this book?

Allow me to introduce myself by telling you what I said at that networking event back in the spring. Remember I had about 50 people watching me and I was allowed only 50 seconds. So I was speaking faster than I would normally do.

I began by saying: "Hi, I'm Rob Yeung, an organizational psychologist, which means that I develop leaders and their teams to do

4

their jobs better by running workshops on leadership, team effectiveness and particular skill topics. For example, I was working on Tuesday with a corporate sales manager and his team at a growing business.

"They do most of their selling to their corporate clients face-to-face. So I was running the second of three workshops designed to help them to present better. To pitch, to get their messages across. To be more memorable and ultimately land more deals. At each session I present a few new principles then the team gets to practise by putting together and then delivering impromptu speeches."

On that day, I gave just one example of the kind of workshop I've run as an organizational psychologist. Actually, I describe myself as an organizational psychologist but you could equally call me a coach, a trainer, a corporate consultant, a keynote speaker, a lecturer. I train managers. I act as a sounding board to business owners. I speak at conferences all over the world to audiences of hundreds or even thousands of people. I lecture at universities and business schools. I work with charities that want to learn to raise funds more effectively. Ultimately, I teach people techniques that will make them better in whatever their walk of life.

Of course there are many books written by consultants. But I hope I'm different from most. I completed a PhD in psychology. So I spent three solid years of doctoral research reading scientific paper after scientific paper as well as getting a few of my own research articles published in technical journals.

The main thing I learnt was the importance of systematic evidence. That we need to have *proof* about what works and what doesn't when it comes to recommending practices and interventions that affect people's lives.

We need to have *proof* about what works and what doesn't.

5

Scientists have long understood that there is something called a "placebo effect". In medical trials, doctors have discovered they can give patients a sham treatment – such as a pill containing nothing more than common household sugar – and yet some patients will feel better.

As a result, any pharmaceutical company wishing to launch a new drug has to prove it has genuine effects over and above those of a sham treatment. In a carefully controlled experiment, some patients are given the new drug while other patients are given the sham treatment. After perhaps weeks, months or even years, researchers then measure the symptoms of those given the drug (the experimental group) against the symptoms of those given the sham treatment (the control group). Only if those in the experimental group have improved significantly more than those in the control group can the drug be considered a success.

The same test can be applied to the recommendations and rituals proposed by corporate consultants, life coaches and other alleged advisers. After all, if they say that they can change your life, shouldn't they be able to prove it?

For example, suppose you meet a friend of a friend at a party. She says that she is a hypnototherapist. It's not just standard old hypnotherapy, she explains. Hypnototherapy is a fantastic new technique which can deliver astonishing results in only a handful of hours. She says that she can hypnotize you into becoming more confident, more engaging and more credible in both your professional and personal life.

She says that it will only take three sessions. And that each session will cost £100.

You pay up. You go along to get hypnotized. And afterwards you feel pretty positive about yourself. But did it really work? Or was it merely a sham treatment which triggered some kind of placebo effect in you? Would you perhaps have been better off spending your £300 and three hours of your time on some other form of coaching or reading books or even just sitting quietly and making plans by yourself, for instance?

In my work as an organizational psychologist, I'm a sceptic. I'm wary of gurus and advisers who claim that they can work miracles. Before recommending anything, I like to have proof. I like to read a research journal and know that a reputable group of scientists at a top university or business school has actually done a study to see what genuinely helped people. So rather than simply telling people what I feel has worked for me personally, I try as far as possible to recommend only techniques that have been revealed by researchers to work for most everyone.

Navigating through this book

So in this book I present you with proven techniques, exercises and advice. I'll show you how psychologists, economists and other scientific sleuths worked out what works and what doesn't. I'll walk you through some of their studies and include detailed references at the end of the book if you wish to follow up further.

We'll look at some of these principles and recommendations in action too. In my work as an organizational psychologist, I encounter countless fascinating and remarkable people. I work with business owners running multi-million-pound businesses, superstar salespeople and award-winning television producers. Women and men who have made a difference and who, well, stand out. And I'm grateful that many of them have imparted their stories in this very book.

Most of these people kindly allowed me to use their real names and talk about the businesses where they work. A few asked me to alter a few identifying details to preserve their anonymity. But all have shared their triumphs, their mistakes and the lessons they've learnt along the way. And by hearing their real-life stories, I hope you will be inspired to try out the techniques within this book too.

What exactly is covered in the book? Allow me to give you an overview by sharing with you a picture. When I'm running workshops, I frequently put up a slide that I call the "influence iceberg". Often, we describe standout people as having charisma or influence. We say that they make an impact, that they possess charm or presence. And these form the tip of the iceberg, the visible part.

Beneath the surface, we can't see the many, many pieces that make up standout individuals. But make no mistake: there are many parts indeed that can be analysed, understood and learnt – and it is these that we will be scrutinizing in this book.

I've structured the book into four main chapters and a conclusion. Here's what's in each and why.

Chapter 1: Boosting Self-belief and Debunking the Confidence Con

We'll start in Chapter 1 on the topic of self-belief. It may sound obvious to say that in order for others to believe in you, you need to believe in yourself. You can't stand out and impress the world unless you have a fairly decent opinion of yourself, right?

Not necessarily. It turns out that the truth is more complex than that. Many standout people actually don't have bucket loads of confidence and I'll tell you some of their surprising stories: a sales manager who hates selling, a business founder wracked by self-doubt, a public relations guru who fears public speaking. However, they all *appear* to be confident, accomplished individuals. They *seem* as if they are able to do great things; and that outward demeanour is often enough to carry them through to great things. So in Chapter 1 we will explore this seeming contradiction – what I call the confidence con – and delve into the secret psychology of becoming more confident.

But allow me to jump ahead for a moment to the good news: there are proven mental manoeuvres that we can all use to feel more confident – some of which take *only seconds* to put into practice. Yes, you read that right. Whether at work or play, there are things we can do ever so quickly that can help us to appear more professional, capable and persuasive to those around us.

Many standout people actually don't have bucket loads of confidence.

Chapter 2: Persuading through Body Language and Nonverbal Communication

You can sometimes spot standout individuals even before they've opened their mouths to speak. There's definitely something about their stance, the way they move, the way they lock eyes with people around them. So in Chapter 2, we will examine the psychology of nonverbal communication. Body language encompasses how we move our bodies and use our hands as well as our facial expressions. But nonverbal communication is body language plus everything about our voices – such as our pacing, loudness and pitch.

When it comes to making an impact, should we speak quickly or slowly? If our aim is to appear more charismatic, should we gesture with our hands more or less? Or is it the type of gestures that make the difference? These questions – and more – will be tackled in this chapter.

A lot has been written about body language which is frankly rubbish.

A lot has been written about body language which is frankly rubbish. So I'll tell you about some of the most recent findings by scientists at the forefront of this field. And we'll learn that even turning your hands palms up or palms down can have different effects on the people around you.

Chapter 3: Winning with Words

In our third chapter, we'll continue our journey by looking at the words, phrases and other verbal tricks that standout people use to make themselves unforgettable and persuasive. What do superstar speakers – ranging from presidents and prime ministers to chief executives and even religious leaders – actually say?

We'll examine how people use tools such as metaphor, visionary statements, autobiographical stories and moral arguments to craft more memorable missives. We'll also take a long look at how speakers can deploy emotions – such as pride and shame, excitement and fear, for instance – to nudge people into action.

When should you use the word "I" rather than the word "we"? And when should you talk about "thinking" as opposed to "feeling"?

These may seem tiny, trivial distinctions. But we'll look at forensic studies demonstrating that even subtle changes of wording can sometimes make a real difference.

In this, the longest chapter in the book, we'll explore both academic studies and real-world examples of how superstar orators, entrepreneurs, salespeople and captains of industry use verbal techniques to help their messages hit home. For example, we'll see how a badly worded email cemented the downfall of one of the most successful companies of the 21st century. And we'll discover how the cheesy saying "If you can believe, you can achieve" may just have merit after all.

Even subtle changes of wording can sometimes make a real difference.

Chapter 4: Augmenting Performance through Passion

When I first floated the idea of a book about standout individuals to friends, colleagues and clients, I heard occasional concerns: the book would be about the triumph of style over substance. It would simply teach people to promote themselves and suck up attention even if they didn't have the underlying skills or capabilities to back anything up.

One of my clients wondered: "Doesn't the notion of standing out play into the hands of self-promoters who talk a good game but never produce the goods?"

But most stellar individuals make their mark because they manage to deliver results, because they're actually good at their jobs. And Chapter 4 will focus squarely on how people stand out by doing sensational work and making things happen.

Most stellar individuals make their mark because they manage to deliver results.

Here's another way of putting it: the first three chapters will look at inspiring and moving others. But this fourth chapter will concentrate on how people inspire and move themselves, as studies tell us that people who enjoy what they do tend to perform better than those who don't. So how can all of us find a place in the world that allows us to feel that little bit more enthusiastic about our working lives?

Conclusions: Onwards, Upwards and Over to You

By the time we near the end of our excursion, we will have scrutinized dozens of research studies conducted by the brightest minds on the planet; we will have delved into the lives of many fascinating individuals. You will be armed with enough tools and techniques to keep you busy for months.

But this book isn't meant to be a dry, academic tome to be read and then set aside, never to be picked up again. I really hope this is a book you will use. That you will apply the principles and practices to overhaul how you use language and behave. That you will think more deeply about the audiences you will address. That you will interact with people in ways that will allow you to be influential and effective.

So in this final section of the book, we'll look at how to take those techniques and recommendations and translate them into a plan of action. I won't have done my job unless you decide to do something differently.

But I'm talking about the end of the book and we haven't really begun yet. So let us start at the beginning by looking at the conundrum of confidence. Why does telling yourself to calm down not work? Why should you sit down to write an essay before your next job interview or a hot date? And how could understanding that your skull isn't made of glass help you to appear more confident and persuasive?

I really hope this is a book you will apply.

12

1

Boosting Self-belief and Debunking the Confidence Con

I learnt that courage was not the absence of fear,
but the triumph over it.
Nelson Mandela

Could you get turned down dozens of times every day, week after week after week, year after year?

I couldn't. In fact, when I was at university and needed a temporary job, I tried my hand at telephone sales.

I lasted one day.

But that's the reality of life for most salespeople. And that's why it takes bundles of confidence to approach dozens or maybe even hundreds of people every single day and get knocked back by most of them.

13

Permit me to introduce you to a dogged sales manager I'll call Julia Kryger. I clearly remember the first time we met because I wondered if she might be trouble. I was running a workshop – the first of five leadership development boot camps – and she was one of the half-dozen senior managers I was working with.

Nearly everyone else in the workshop seemed chatty, friendly, engaged. They listened attentively as I presented. They reflected on the questions I asked them. They took part in the discussions and raised sensible queries. But not Kryger.

She sat with her legs crossed, checked her smartphone every few minutes and said almost nothing. With her tanned, athletic frame and North American accent, I imagined she was probably a cheerleader or even a mean girl at school. She came across as aloof, tough and iron-lady confident. I wondered if she might be a sceptic, thinking she already knew it all or didn't believe that leadership was a teachable discipline.

Fast forward nearly a year and she laughed warmly as I shared my recollections of my first impressions of her.

"If you were to do a survey of my colleagues, they would probably say that I'm one of the most confident people in the business. They would describe me as really ambitious, confident, on it, quite matter of fact, very business oriented, just like a bulldozer," she told me.

Kryger is Head of International Sales for a UK-based "audience technology" start-up. The fledgling business uses clever algorithms to help advertisers target people online. Within the space of just over a year, she has already recruited a sales squad of three people who report to her and she has landed deals with top brands, including Adidas, British Airways, Volkswagen and Marriott Hotels, to the tune of £2 million. She's the youngest person on the management board too. Not bad for a 28-year-old.

"I say this not to toot my own horn but I do feel I've excelled really quickly. I've moved up the ranks pretty quickly and on minimal experience," she said.

She had just got back from a business trip to Germany where she and her boss were pitching to a major advertiser. She was in France and the Netherlands not long before that too. Clearly, she's the kind of strong-willed individual who just loves high pressure and landing big deals, right?

"Even [my boss] said this to me: 'You must love presenting in front of a room full of people. You're like this power woman. You eat people alive.'"

But it's an impression that conceals an emotional battle raging secretly within her. Only a handful of her closest compatriots know that she has wrestled greatly with fear, suffered overwhelming panic attacks and has even sought medical help for anxiety-related health issues.

"There are people that mask anxiety really well and others that cower and hide and I'm definitely one of those people that puts on a face when I walk in the door at work," she admitted.

There are people that mask anxiety really well and others that cower and hide.

Kryger experienced her first panic attack three months into her current role. Ironically, her boss had that day told her how proud he was of her rapid success. He had initially set her a target of bringing in £25,000 of revenue and she had brought in over £50,000.

In celebration, she went shopping for a new pair of jeans in Top Shop when she suddenly noticed that she felt really "spaced out". She rushed home with the sense that something terrible was happening. The moment she walked through the door, she was hit by a wave of new crippling sensations. She was so scared that she asked her flatmate to phone for an ambulance.

"I thought I was dying," she remembered.

Later, a doctor explained that she had experienced a panic attack. Unfortunately, it wouldn't be her last.

Like many people, she experiences the greatest anxiety when she feels she is being judged. That's tough given that, as a representative for her business, she is naturally being scrutinized by every prospective client she meets.

"Sitting down in a board room can produce a physical response in me that's almost like I'm fighting my body. Elevated heart rate, shortness of breath, sometimes fully fledged panic," she said.

"It's not the kind of job where you come in and you have a job description and a daily to-do list. It's being in the middle of this massive, fabulous storm that you're incredibly passionate about, but that can be quite overwhelming. So overwhelming," she continued.

Advertisers often pull out with little notice, leaving the business with gaping black holes in its finances. When that happens, she has to scramble to bring in sales from elsewhere.

"There are days when I feel like I'm really on top of my game but it's like the more success I have, the more the pressure mounts. And I can't live up to this. The bar just gets set higher and higher – if that makes any sense?"

She understands that the pressure doesn't come from her boss. She is savvy enough to recognize it comes from herself – that the standards by which she judges herself are far tougher than those of her workmates or clients. When she does make the smallest mistake or gaffe, she punishes herself more harshly than anyone else, too.

The easy option would be to quit and seek a less tempestuous, more predictable job, perhaps working for a large, established corporate media business rather than a fiery young start-up. But no, she is determined to soothe the madhouse of her emotions.

Over the last year, she has worked on her confidence. As well as making lifestyle alterations – cutting out caffeine and alcohol, exercising more and meditating – she has sought the counsel of a psychologist and regularly practises mindfulness techniques.

She has learnt to divorce her personal identity from her professional highs and lows. Yes, a bad meeting with a client may hurt. But it's still only a job. It may make her feel anxious, but there's nothing there that can physically harm her. It's not the end of the world.

"There's two ways that you can look at it," she concluded. "You can either be one of those people who shrivels in a corner and says, 'I can't do it, I'm going to give up' or you're the type of person like me who tries to calm this inner shaky little lamb."

So don't expect Kryger to chicken out of the fight any time soon. She is growing her department by grooming the next generation of talent. She is working with some of the most enviable brands in the world. She has calmed the shaky little lamb inside her and may one day turn it into a tiger.

Being both successful and scared

Julia Kryger is succeeding *in spite* of how she feels. And you may be surprised to learn how very many people are in exactly the same situation.

Take north-London-born singer-songwriter Adele as a rather famous example. Despite having released her debut album only in 2008, she already has an enviable collection of awards and even world records to her name. Her 2011 album *21* topped the chart in more than 30 countries.

The first time I really noticed her was when watching her sing *Someone Like You* at the British music industry BRIT Awards in February 2011. Singing live under a spotlight accompanied only by a pianist, she cast a spell over an audience of thousands of the British public as well as hundreds of music producers, record label heads and other industry bigwigs. Her emotionally raw performance was possibly the highlight of the award show.

As I write this sentence, the YouTube video has racked up over 156 million views. Tap the words "Adele performing *Someone Like You* BRIT Awards 2011" into YouTube and you'll find the video.[1] Despite the less-than-perfect sound quality and the slight graininess of the images, I defy you to watch the performance and not be mesmerized.

So does she sing effortlessly? No. In an interview with *Rolling Stone* magazine, she confessed: "I'm scared of audiences. I get shitty scared. One show in Amsterdam, I was so nervous I escaped out the fire exit. I've thrown up a couple of times. Once in Brussels, I projectile-vomited on someone. I just gotta bear it. But I don't like touring. I have anxiety attacks a lot."[2]

Despite feeling anxious, she has managed to get on with her singing career. She even won an Academy Award for the theme song to the 2013 James Bond movie *Skyfall*.

In fact, there are many actors, performers and entertainers who suffer great fretfulness: actors Sir Derek Jacobi and Dame Judi Dench, the comedian and TV presenter Stephen Fry, to name but a few. But they all get on with it anyway.

Then there's a client of mine, a 50-something advertising executive who admitted that he was wracked with insecurity. He frequently woke at four or five o'clock in the morning obsessing about the tasks that he had to do the next day. Yet he had created some of the most talked-about advertising campaigns of the 21st century.

Understanding the confidence con

We'll encounter further examples of successful but less than entirely confident individuals throughout this chapter. All of them – famous and less famous – have succeeded in spite of their fears, their doubts, their worries. And they all illustrate what I call the confidence con: the external appearance of confidence in others deceives us into believing that they feel confident internally. The reality is that people often appear confident by how they behave publicly but can be afflicted by anxiety and doubt privately.

People often appear confident by how they behave publicly but can be afflicted by anxiety and doubt privately.

It's a terrible state of affairs because it isolates the innumerable people who feel less than 100 per cent confident. When we feel worry, doubt or even dread and outright panic, we are conned into believing that we're alone, that we're losers and that few others can feel the same way.

But that's not the case, as demonstrated by scientific surveys. For example, a posse of social scientists led by Alexander Jordan at the Tuck School of Business conducted a nifty series of studies delving into this very issue. In an enlightening study, they asked participants to guess the extent to which their friends experienced negative emotions such as sadness and anxiety. The scientists then asked their friends to disclose their actual emotional experiences.

Immediately, the researchers spotted a clear disconnect. Most participants underestimated their friends' negative emotions by 17.2 per cent. In other words, most of us probably feel that our friends are nearly 20 per cent less unhappy than they actually are. On average, other people are almost 20 per cent more anxious, lonelier and more distressed than you think.[3]

Other people are almost 20 per cent more anxious, lonelier and more distressed than you think.

Why does this happen?

It doesn't help that most of us are socialized to believe we shouldn't reveal exactly how bad we feel. Alexander Jordan's group calls this "the preferential suppression of negative emotion". Unspoken rules dictate that it's fine to showcase positive emotions such as enthusiasm or joy – we're allowed to laugh, whoop and celebrate life's pleasures – but those same unspoken guidelines discourage us from being killjoys; so in public we tend to downplay our worry, loneliness and frustration.

As a result, Jordan's team makes the case that most of us live in a state of "pluralistic emotional ignorance". We are blind to the true feelings of those around us. We underestimate the extent to which others feel the same way. And if you think other people are less anxious and unhappy than they actually are, you may fall into the trap of believing that the rest of the world is calmer, happier and more confident than you.

So remember, remember, remember: many standout individuals appear unruffled on the surface while being shredded internally by nervousness or worries.

If that's the case, then what does the path to success look like? Well, I believe that achieving anything comes from taking appropriate action however challenging it may feel at the time. It's about doing what's needed in order to pursue your long-term goals, even if taking action feels rather worrying or uncertain in the short term.

So, sure, you may be anxious about having to give a presentation to colleagues, but you do it *in spite* of your worries. Or you fear rejection when asking that attractive person out but you do it *regardless* of how you feel.

This certainly applied to Julia Kryger, the sales chief we encountered at the start of the chapter. She feels gripped by fears and anxieties about her work. But despite her inner turmoil, she gets on with her high-pressure job, pitches to clients and pushes herself.

Many standout individuals appear unruffled on the surface while being shredded internally by nervousness.

But the good news is that there are ways to quell unruly feelings and jumpstart our confidence. So let's look at what the latest science has to say about combating nerves and building the kind of standout demeanour that might help us all achieve our goals.

Performing mind over matter

Every day, we and so many people around us are confronted by anxiety-provoking situations. Consider some of the following that I came across in just the last month or so:

- Anwen, a 17-year-old daughter of a friend and would-be concert pianist, is about to play three technically demanding pieces of music to a panel of musical connoisseurs who have gathered from all around the country. If she performs well, she may be offered a scholarship at a prestigious school of music. If she fumbles things, her dreams of a future in music may be crushed.

21

- Eric is a finance manager in his early 50s. He worked for a major oil and gas company for over 25 years but was made redundant well over a year ago. Despite having applied for dozens of jobs, he has been invited to only a handful of interviews and has received only fairly menial job offers so far. He fears that recruiters consider him too old to be employable. A friend has personally recommended him for a role and he is now waiting in the lobby of his potential new employer, about to be interviewed by the chief financial officer of the company. He feels that this could be his last chance of finding meaningful employment.
- Susannah, a shy human resources executive in her late 20s, has been chosen to give a 10-minute presentation on behalf of her department at the company's quarterly conference. There will be a crowd of nearly 120 in the audience, including the chief executive and all of the directors of the business. She worries every time she has to give a presentation and feels nervous when speaking in front of even a half-dozen workmates. And in less than 24 hours she will have to speak in front of the largest audience of her life.

In those critical moments, what advice would you give these three individuals? Would you perhaps recommend they try to relax and calm down?

If so, you would be in splendid company. When Harvard Business School professor Alison Wood Brooks surveyed 300 people, she found that the vast majority – 84.9 per cent, in fact – said they would encourage anxious friends or co-workers to relax and calm down.

Trying to calm down may be rather terrible advice.

That's sensible guidance right?

Actually, no. It's very badly wrong. It turns out that trying to calm down may be rather terrible advice.

A rising star in the research firmament, Brooks formulated a cunning experiment to test the effects of different instructions on the anxiety levels of 140 participants. She began by explaining to all of them that they would be given a couple of minutes to prepare a two-minute persuasive speech on the topic "Why you are a good work partner". The participants were told that their speeches would be both delivered to an experimenter and recorded for scrutiny later by a committee.

Immediately before delivering their speeches, the participants were split into two groups and told to repeat either:

- "I am calm."
- "I am excited."

Immediately after the presentations, Brooks asked the participants how they felt and found that both groups reported feeling equally uneasy. Neither instruction helped to diminish their anxiety.

However, the difference was clearly detectable when she showed the video recordings to three independent judges who hadn't been present at the actual presentations. The participants who had said to themselves "I am excited" were rated more highly in just about every conceivable way. These speakers who tried to get fired up were judged to be more competent, more confident and more persuasive than those who had told themselves "I am calm."[4]

This finding clearly has profound implications for would-be public speakers. Don't try to calm down. Tell yourself you're excited instead.

Why doesn't trying to calm down work? Psychologists categorize emotions along two different dimensions. One of these dimensions is the valence of an emotion. So feelings such as contentment, exhilaration and optimism are positive emotions. Guilt, shame, anxiety and frustration are negative emotions.

The other dimension is the physiological arousal associated with the emotion. So both excitement and anxiety are characterized by high arousal – that means a pounding heart rate, faster breathing, perhaps a sensation of sweatiness and so on. On the other hand, emotions such as sadness and contentment are associated with low arousal – these emotions slow us down.

Plotting valence versus arousal gives us a two-by-two matrix of the types of emotion that we can feel:

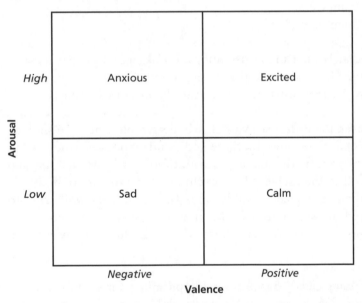

You can see that feeling anxious is both high arousal and has a negative valence. Attempting to turn anxiety into calmness means having to move across two categories – it involves both trying to shift from a negative to a positive valence as well as having to reduce the arousal from high to low.

But now look at where excitement sits in the matrix. Both excitement and anxiety are already high-arousal emotions. So turning anxiety into elation involves moving across only one boundary – from a negative to a positive valence. And that seems easier for our mental operating systems to handle.

Putting it another way, trying to steer our emotional state from anxious to calm is like making a 180-degree turn in a car at high speed. It's nigh on impossible. But making the shift from anxious to excited is more like a sharp 90-degree turn and eminently more doable.

I recently applied this particular technique to exquisite effect. I don't feel anxious giving presentations, but there was one situation that scared me: the thought of having laser eye surgery to correct short-sightedness.

For most of my life since my late teens, I wore glasses or contact lenses. I was so short-sighted that I struggled to see objects that were further than an arm's reach away from me. I couldn't cross the road safely because I couldn't see cars. I couldn't even sit on the sofa and watch TV – all the faces blurred and I couldn't tell who was speaking.

I had been mulling over laser eye surgery for about 10 years. But I was deeply apprehensive. Reading about the operation, I learnt that the surgeon clamps your eyelids open, applies a suction device to the eyeball and cuts a flap in the front of the eyeball. All of that sounded bad enough. And that's all before the laser fires up and starts vaporizing – yes, literally vaporizing – your eye. Some patients say they can actually smell burning. And you're awake, fully conscious throughout the whole ordeal.

But eventually I decided to at least have an initial meeting with a surgeon. And in order to keep my anxiety at bay during all of the consultations and even the surgery itself, I told myself that I was excited. I kept thinking about all of the benefits of not having to wear glasses and being able to discard my contact lenses.

Don't try to calm down. Tell yourself you're excited instead.

It worked. I hardly felt anxious. I was a model patient and I even weirdly quite enjoyed the surgery itself! And all because I kept telling myself "I'm excited."

Dispelling illusions

If you've ever felt worried or scared about anything in life, remember that you're not alone. In fact, you're probably surrounded by folks just like you.

We already discussed the confidence con: the fact that the fears of others aren't readily visible to us. You categorically can't see into other people's heads to know what they're actually feeling. Conversely, though, we worry that the crowd around us *can* see into our own heads.

Take an individual I know who I'll call Ralph Dixon. A slim 35-year-old with a wholesome air and a genial smile, he strikes me as likeable, grounded, confident – even a tad cocky. I could imagine him being cast in an American TV drama as the lead character's best buddy or a good cop.

"Day to day, I have no issue in social situations, meeting new people and sharing my experience, thinking about things to talk about," he explained in a languid drawl.

As I listened to him speak about his career, I built up a picture of him as a bit of a hotshot. When he was in his 20s, he applied for a job that specifically asked for candidates with seven plus years of experience. He only had two-and-a-bit years of experience at the time but he applied anyway. He got the job.

Now he's a founder and director for a technology start-up. The business started up less than three years ago and has just over a dozen employees. As an investor in the business, he's on course to make his millions before he turns 40 should things continue to go well.

"I've always wanted to be an entrepreneur," he told me.

"That means you have to envision a certain amount of success for yourself with a huge, huge, huge high probability of failure. You know when you start in business that you have an 85 per cent chance of failure or probably higher."

To add to the pressure, he has a family who depend on him. He is supporting his wife and a two-year-old son. Rather than being able to buy a house, he has staked his savings on his business venture working out.

That's confidence in abundance, right? Not everyone could cope with the pressure of putting their life's savings in a business and betting that it will pay off.

But what the world can't see is the doubts that he faces on the job. When his work goes well, he's calm and collected. But when he feels too stretched or projects fail, he has his doubts.

"You get a voice that says, 'You can't do it. You're not going to be successful. You're going to fail. Things aren't working in this, this, this and this area. It's too hard. It's not for me. You can't do it. You're not smart enough.'"

A major worry of his is what his buddies and his peers would think of him should he screw up. Like most people, he can't help but want to be successful in the eyes of those around him.

"One of the things my wife pointed out to me is that [I have] this desire to prove to everyone that I'm successful," he added.

"If your peers don't feel you're successful, then you get really upset about that." He pauses, his mind drifting to some darker place. "Get really upset."

On the surface, hardly anyone can detect the upheaval within Dixon. He confides in a tiny circle of his most trusted confidants – he says he has only three individuals in this inner circle. However, to the rest of the world he continues to appear gregarious, focused and effective in his work. It's only in the unseen places of his own mind that the doubts can have him in a spin.

Thankfully, he has come to realize that he isn't the only person in the world to feel this way. He understands that confidence can often be a mask that people wear in public even though they may privately be feeling tremendously burdened and completely fraught.

"You could look at the most successful people and they appear to be the most confident people and that they've always been that way," he said.

"I just don't believe that's true. I think we're all human and we all suffer from moments of self-doubt and issues like that."

We're tricked into believing that everyone else must feel more confident than we do.

Sage words indeed. *We're all human. We all suffer from moments of self-doubt.* These words apply to so, so many successful individuals. They appear confident on the surface. But that's all it is: the *appearance* of confidence. We can't know how they're feeling. Dixon is another example of the confidence con: that we're tricked into believing that everyone else must

28

feel more confident than we do – simply because we judge them on their appearance, their behaviour, how they seem outwardly.

Think about your own experience when you're giving a big presentation or speaking in public. Think back to a really huge event. Maybe having to speak at your best friend's wedding or a presentation to a roomful of bigwigs. What goes through your mind when you're feeling nervous? Perhaps you can feel your heart pounding. You may notice how dry your mouth feels but at the same time how sweaty your palms are. Does that make you worry more that the audience can see how edgy you are – and that they will therefore take you less seriously?

Or say you're on a date with an attractive lady or gentleman but quivering inside that you'll say or do something wrong. When there's an awkward silence in the conversation or you make a comment that doesn't go down well, do you worry that the object of your affection can tell how nervous you are?

Our physical sensations are so vivid. The thoughts and feelings crashing around in our heads are so rampant. It's perfectly natural to worry that we're more nervous than the rest of the world – and that they can detect how we're feeling.

However, a psychological saviour and professor at Cornell University, Thomas Gilovich, has documented across numerous studies that most of us overestimate the extent to which other people can sense how we're really feeling. He calls this effect the "illusion of transparency": a belief that our thoughts, feelings and emotions are more apparent to others than is actually the case.[5]

In one experiment, Gilovich asked pairs of volunteers to give three-minute presentations to each other. To illustrate how it worked, let's

Most of us overestimate the extent to which other people can sense how we're really feeling.

29

walk through what may have happened to one pairing that we'll call Beatrice and Sukesh.

Gilovich explains to the pair that the study is about impromptu public speaking. He explains that he will flip a coin to choose one of the two. That person will then have to go to the front of the room and stand at a podium to deliver a speech on one of two topics. The topic will be handed to him or her on a piece of card.

Gilovich flips the coin and Beatrice wins – or loses, depending on how you look at it. She has to go first.

She moves to the front of the room and is handed a card saying "The best and worst things about life today". And with no further time to prepare, she has to give a three-minute speech on her allotted topic.

Immediately after she has finished, it's over to Sukesh. He gets given a different card saying "The most important moral lessons to teach one's children". Again, he has to speak immediately and for three minutes.

Immediately afterwards, both Beatrice and Sukesh are escorted to separate cubicles to complete a short questionnaire rating not only how nervous they felt but also how nervous they thought the other person looked.

At the end of the questionnaire, they are also asked to tick one of two statements:

- "I appeared more nervous than the other participant."
- "The other participant appeared more nervous than I did."

When Gilovich ran this experiment with 20 pairs of volunteers, he found that the vast majority of participants ticked the first statement, believing that he or she was more nervous than the other person. More interestingly, though, in 40 per cent of the pairs, *both* participants ticked the first statement, believing that they had appeared more nervous than the other person.

That would be like Beatrice believing she was the more nervous performer while at the same time Sukesh knowing with full certainty that he was the more nervous of the two. Clearly, both individuals in a pair can't have been more nervous. So that means that a significant proportion of people massively overestimate how nervous they appear to others.

That's excellent news for a start. We may believe in the illusion of transparency but the key word here is "illusion". It's not true that we are transparent, that our true sentiments are as visible as we may feel. Translation: we probably *appear* less nervous than we *feel*.

I think of the confidence con and the illusion of transparency as being two sides of the same coin. The confidence con leads us to believe that other people are more confident than we are – that their outward appearance of confidence must mean they feel confident inwardly too. On the other hand, the illusion of transparency leads us to believe that our *lack* of confidence is more visible to others than it is.

We probably *appear* less nervous than we *feel*.

When running workshops on confidence, I often show a single slide that neatly summarizes the tragic repercussions of these two states of mind. As you can see, Sukesh believes his anxiety must be noticeable, which only makes him more tense. But his nervousness isn't actually as readily apparent to Beatrice as he reckons, so poor Beatrice believes that she is the nervier of the two. So everybody loses.

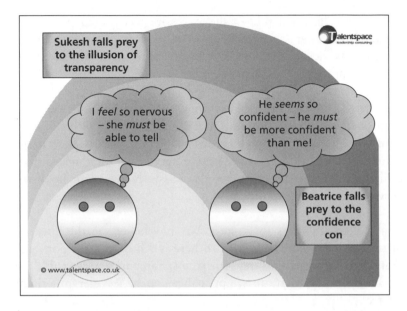

Sukesh falls prey to the illusion of transparency

I *feel* so nervous – she *must* be able to tell

He *seems* so confident – he *must* be more confident than me!

Beatrice falls prey to the confidence con

© www.talentspace.co.uk

But let's focus for now on the illusion of transparency. If we think about it more carefully, the fact that we may feel more anxious than we seem to others may not actually be so surprising. After all, when we can feel our trepidation, we may worry that it is visible in our body language: the slight shake of our hands, perhaps the look on our faces or even a tone of uncertainty in our voices.

Regrettably, obsessing about how worried we look can trigger a downward spiral. It can make us worry even more.

Mercifully, there is a solution. In a follow-up experiment, Gilovich and a collaborator took several dozen students and randomly assigned them to one of two groups. The first (experimental) group read a paragraph about the illusion of transparency. The second (control) group read a paragraph telling them that it was natural to feel nervous and wishing them good luck.

Participants in each group were videoed giving three-minute presentations and then debriefed as to how they felt. Interestingly, participants in the experimental group felt just as nervous as those in the control group. Informing them about the illusion of transparency had *not* made them feel less nervous.

Huh? What's going on? How does this supposed illusion of transparency help us – if at all?

Here's the useful bit. When the researchers showed the videos to viewers who had not been present at the video recordings, they found that these independent observers tended to rate the presentations of participants from the experimental group more highly than the presentations of control participants.

In other words, understanding the illusion of transparency helped experimental participants deliver objectively better presentations *in spite* of how nervous they still felt. Perhaps even more remarkably, the onlookers rated the speeches of experimental participants 20.9 per cent more highly than those in the control group – that's a fairly impressive improvement for an intervention that takes only minutes to perform.

Audiences can't pick up on your anxiety as well as you might expect.

Giving yourself an instant communications boost

To be clear then: understanding the illusion of transparency will not necessarily make you feel any less nervous. However, it can help you deliver a show-stopping presentation or be a better date or conversationalist in spite of how you feel. And all you have to do is read the following paragraph that Gilovich and his fellow investigator Kenneth Savitsky shared with participants:

I think it may help you to know that research has found that audiences can't pick up on your anxiety as well as

(Continued)

33

you might expect. Psychologists have documented what is called an "illusion of transparency". Those speaking feel that their nervousness is transparent, but in reality their feelings are not so apparent to observers. This happens because our own emotional experience can be so strong, we are sure our emotions "leak out". In fact, observers aren't as good at picking up on a speaker's emotional state as we tend to expect. So, while you might be so nervous you're convinced that everyone else can tell how nervous you are, in reality that's very rarely the case. What's inside of you typically manifests itself too subtly to be detected by others. With this in mind, you should just try to relax and try to do your best. Know that if you become nervous, you'll probably be the only one to know.

So this may come in handy the next time you have to perform in front of an audience – whether that's an audience of one or a hundred. Just re-read this paragraph and remind yourself that you are *not* transparent.

Powering through job interviews

As an organizational psychologist, I often get asked to tutor job hunters, to prep them to cope with the onslaught of questions that may come during a job interview. It's probably the single most common issue that clients raise with me in one-to-one coaching.

Take a client of mine I'll call Lucy Grimes, for example. A modest woman in her forties who had spent over 10 years working contentedly enough as a marketing manager for a private healthcare provider, she unexpectedly found herself out of a job. With less than a month's notice, her department was restructured. She and over a dozen colleagues were hastily paid off and found themselves looking for new jobs.

She had a solid track record in planning and running events so she got invited to a fair few interviews. But she just wasn't getting any offers. Neither did she know where she was going wrong. Despite her best efforts to ask for feedback from interviewers on why she wasn't successful, she found that interviewers simply weren't interested in furnishing her with constructive criticism. As a result, her confidence was slipping and she didn't quite know how to turn matters around.

Of course her situation is hardly unique. The **Could simply** job interview can be a scary situation for many *feeling* **more in** people. And that's hardly surprising. There **control boost** could be any number of other candidates vying **your chances of** for the position. It's a competition in which **getting an** there will be many losers but only one winner. **offer?**

And we all know that interviewers can be somewhat capricious in their decision-making. No matter how much experience you may have and how well qualified you may be, even the smallest blunder can spell rejection. You're being judged on everything you say, how you come across, even what you're wearing and *who you are*. Ultimately, no matter how badly you may covet the job, it's totally and completely out of your control whether you will be offered it.

But could simply *feeling* more in control boost your chances of getting an offer?

This was the quandary that social and political psychologist Joris Lammers of the University of Cologne in Germany set out to answer in collaboration with a cadre of international collaborators from business schools in both France and the United States. The

35

team gathered together a group of undergraduate students who wanted to apply for entry to business school and invited these participants to attend mock interviews by expert interviewers as part of their preparation for their real business school interviews.

Just prior to the interview, the participants were split into one of three groups:

- The first group was asked to spend a few minutes writing about a situation in which they had felt powerful.
- The second group was asked to spend a few minutes writing about a situation in which they had felt powerless.
- The third group acted as a control and was given no further special instructions.

The interviewers were not told which participants had been given which set of instructions. These specialist interviewers were merely told to grill the candidates hard and then answer a single question: "Would they admit the applicant to business school? Yes or no?"

Remember that these participants were all genuinely applying for entry to business school so they saw these mock interviews as a quintessential part of their preparation. Given the stakes, they were all highly motivated to perform well. But only 47.1 per cent of the participants in the control group passed the interview.

As you can no doubt guess, the participants that wrote about a high power situation did better. How much better? An impressive 68.4 per cent of these participants passed the inter-

Write about a high-power situation and you give yourself a colossal boost.

view. Pity the participants that wrote about feeling powerless, though. Only 26.3 per cent of them passed the interview.[6]

The headline from the study should be clear. Write about a high-power situation – a time when

36

you had influence and control over another person or persons – and you give yourself a colossal boost. You put yourself into the right frame of mind: you feel strong, in control, confident.

Now, you may be wondering why the instigators of the study included a group in which participants wrote about a time they felt powerless. Clearly, no one would voluntarily spend five minutes immediately prior to a job interview reminding themselves of such a bleak moment.

But in real life many job hunters *do* genuinely feel powerless. The job market of the 21st century has become so competitive that innumerable people have felt hopeless, out of control, unable to get the jobs they feel they deserve. I've coached so many job seekers suffering from flagging levels of confidence, often reeling from the gut punch of having been made redundant in some cases even a year or more previously. I've supported individuals returning to work after extended periods of illness and women looking for jobs after having taken years off to raise families. I've worked to buoy the self-confidence of job hunters in just about every occupation and industry you can imagine, from cabin crew for airlines to managing directors in investment banking.

You can understand how easy it is to go into a doom spiral. Get rejected just a handful of times and you start to wonder if something rather fundamental is wrong. Perhaps your skills are out of date. Maybe your experience isn't quite relevant. Maybe you're not being assertive **In real life many job hunters *do* genuinely feel powerless.** enough – or you're being too pushy. Oh no, what if it's your personality that interviewers don't like? So yes, vast numbers of people do feel powerless.

Remember that the study by Lammers and his colleagues found that powerless participants passed the interview only 26.3 per cent

37

of the time. In contrast, participants primed to feel powerful were successful 68.4 per cent of the time. That's a gigantic difference. And all thanks to a mere five-minute intervention.

The researchers wrapped up their research by saying that their discovery "seems to offer hope to millions of job and school applicants around the world – tap into your inner sense of confidence by recalling an experience of power". I couldn't have put it better myself.

Giving yourself a power-up

Doing an exercise to feel more powerful sounds like the kind of rubbishy advice that a self-help quack would recommend. You know: the kind of alleged guru who believes in chanting, psychic energy and harnessing the cosmic forces of the universe. But studies conducted by reputable scientists at top universities and business schools suggest that feeling powerful may have very quantifiable benefits.

For starters, the research does *not* tell us that we should simply repeat over and over again a mantra such as "I am powerful." No, the so-called power priming technique takes at least several minutes of quiet thought and reflection to write what I have dubbed "power paragraphs".

To help you feel powerful when you need it, I recommend a two-stage exercise. The first part is to spend some time thinking about a handful of situations in which you have felt powerful.

Make a short list of three to five different occasions when you had power over another person or persons. That could be at work, at home with your family, socially or in any other situation you choose. The point is simply to make sure you have a handful of powerful situations at the ready for when you may need them.

Then, to stoke your feeling of power – perhaps you have an interview or a crucial meeting coming up – the second part involves writing about one of those situations. Based on objective studies demonstrating the benefits of so-called power priming, use the following instructions the next time you seek to give yourself a shot of confidence:

- Take a few moments to recall a situation in which you had power over another individual or individuals. "Power" is defined as control over the ability of another person (or persons) to get something that he/she/they want. Power could also include being in a position to evaluate someone else.
- Spend five minutes writing about this incident.

Want to know something quite odd, though? Power paragraphs work for written job applications too. Lammers and his conclave of scientists ran a second experiment, this time asking participants to submit written applications for a real job. Participants were, as before, asked to recall and write about a time they felt either powerful or powerless. And then they wrote an application letter for the position before putting the letter in an envelope and handing it over for analysis.

Two recruitment experts waded through all of the letters and judged them on their expressed self-confidence. How confident did each applicant seem – based purely on the written application?

Again, the experimenters were able to detect a small but significant effect of the power paragraph intervention. Participants who first wrote about a time they felt powerful wrote letters that were judged by independent raters as being more self-confident.

39

Gosh.

That, to me, is pretty mind-boggling. You can understand how feeling more powerful during a face-to-face interview will lead to more eye contact, more confident body language and perhaps more assertive dialogue. But in a *written* application?

Even more uncannily, when the scientists tried to understand in what way letters written by power-primed participants were more successful, they couldn't figure out why. The researchers digitally scanned the letters and analysed them for content. The letters of power-primed participants were of the same length as measured in three different ways – the number of sentences, the number of words and the usage of longer, six-or-more letter words. Their letters did not employ the first person singular any more or any less. They did not use any more or less positive language; neither did they utilize any more or less negative language.

I'd love to be able to give you a simple explanation. But that's not the way science always works. The messy truth is that we don't know exactly in what way power helps us to communicate more confidently in writing. Freakishly, it just does.

We can answer another question, though: "Why does feeling powerful help us?"

A whole raft of studies illustrates that the feeling of power – or powerlessness – actually affects the brain's functions. For example, a team led by social psychologist Pamela Smith at Radboud University Nijmegen in the Netherlands demonstrated in one experiment that powerless participants made more mistakes when given computerized tasks to complete than participants who felt more powerful. In a further investigation, the same group also found that powerless participants were less able to make effective plans.[7] Elsewhere, British experimental psychologist Ana Guinote at the

University of Kent has similarly found that powerless participants tend to be more easily distractible.[8]

Taken together, these studies suggest that feeling powerless doesn't just crush motivation – it may actually reduce the ability of our mental machinery to function productively. To use psychological jargon, feeling out of control impairs executive function.

The feeling of power – or powerlessness – actually affects the brain's functions.

Daily life is often characterized by setbacks, rejections and obstacles. A project flops. A colleague blasts you for a mistake. A customer decides to dump you. Your partner chides you yet again for not having done a household chore. Whether such knocks are big or small, conventional wisdom tells us that we should simply dust ourselves off, see them as a necessary part of life and get on with things.

But a convincing body of studies suggest that's not all we should be doing. We may also need to protect our confidence, our sense of being in control and in command of our own destinies. Feeling powerless as a result of the daily grind and little setbacks we experience could have supersized connotations for our ability to be at our best. Don't let that happen to you.

Nurturing deep-rooted confidence

I run a fair number of workshops on confident public speaking and presentations. Some of these are for inexperienced people who need some basic rules to follow; some of these are for veteran sales professionals and executives who want to hone their podium presentations to perfection. But the same question crops up over and over: can people ever truly change? Is confidence really something that can be honed and developed – or are we just born and then stuck forever with either lots or not so much of it?

Confidence is something we can all cultivate. Not long ago, I met a managing director who is a sterling example that our level of confidence isn't something that is immutable and unchangeable. No, confidence is something we can all cultivate.

Claire Mason founded public relations agency Man Bites Dog 10 years ago. Her 30th birthday had been a real milestone. "I thought I have to be brave and it's a now-or-never situation," she told me.

Since then, she has grown the business into a multi-million-pound concern with 30 employees. She lists businesses such as the law firm Linklaters, healthcare business Bupa and technology firm Google amongst her clients.

Mason cuts a tall, imposing figure but this is offset by smiling eyes and a self-deprecating sense of humour. She describes herself as ultra-confident when she's in a room consulting with clients. She can sit with a chief executive and a half-dozen senior executives and happily discuss their business needs and what they must do to continue being successful. That's no trouble for her at all.

As her business grew, though, she was increasingly asked to speak at seminars and conferences to audiences of dozens of people at a time. However, she kept turning them down.

"I started to realize I was being asked to do speaker engagements and I was always finding excuses not to do them," she said.

"So I thought, actually that's not good enough. I wouldn't accept it from a member of my team. I'd ask, 'What support do you need to be comfortable in doing this?' and help them in getting there."

For most of her adult life, Mason had managed to evade any proper public speaking. The first time she spoke, she was racked with anxiety.

"I felt huge amounts of adrenaline, tension. For me, I don't sleep the night before. I can't eat. I feel quite sick. And my calf muscles become really tense so I can't really wear heels if I'm public speaking. I need to feel more grounded," she said.

The thing is: she didn't die. Not even metaphorically. In fact, she was great. When audiences rated her, she was stunned to find out how much they valued hearing her speak.

"I'm scoring 9s and 10s out of 10. So actually, although at the time I might feel I've not done a great job, I must have done better than I thought I had," she added.

She spoke at eight events over 12 months and began to feel less nervous about it. I asked her to rate how nervous she felt on a scale of 1 to 10 at that very first speaking event. Widening her eyes, she said, "10!"

But after just seven more events – and remember that these were the first eight times she had *ever* spoken in public – she said that she'd experienced an 8 out of 10 in terms of her anxiety levels.

Sure, she still feels nervous, but it's beginning to get easier. She's seeing her confidence blossom.

Practice is nature's own beta blocker.

"It gave me confidence to have the evidence that I performed better than I thought I did. I think your own assessment is probably always quite harsh and critical. I would come out thinking about all of the things I hadn't said or missed or perhaps didn't handle as well as I would have liked to have done. But when you see the feedback coming back from other people, actually the feedback was very good."

That's a lesson worth learning by itself: that many of us are more picky and disparaging of our own performances than those of the people around us. But there's another takeaway too.

Whatever your situation, you *can* feel more confident about it.

Mason was 39 years old when she began speaking in public. She had been working for nearly two decades before she decided to tackle her fear of public speaking. And after only eight such events over the course of less than a year she felt noticeably more secure. Practice is nature's own beta blocker.

Over the years I've worked with leaders and executives in charge of guiding businesses and other organizations ranging in size from dozens to thousands of employees. Many of these individuals confessed privately that they dreaded having to stand up and speak. Perhaps, like Mason and countless others, you too feel anxious about standing up in front of crowds and sharing your thoughts. Maybe your bugbear is dating or job interviews. Or networking with strangers, confronting bull-headed people, lecturing students or something else. But whatever your situation, you *can* feel more confident about it. If Mason can do it, so can you.

Mixing and matching to find what works best for you

Being able to speak with confidence is a prerequisite for standing out. You can't make a splash unless people – colleagues, friends, potential romantic partners, whatever – feel comfortable around you. So hopefully I have given you some practical techniques that you can use to hone your confidence and leave people with a great impression.

I recently ran a workshop on the topic of confidence at the Royal College of Physicians, an organization that represents tens of thousands of doctors and medical professionals both in the UK and abroad. We discussed topics such as how to phrase requests assertively but not aggressively. And we covered just two confidence techniques: Alison Wood Brooks' "I am excited" reappraisal technique and Joris Lammers' power paragraphs.

At the end of the workshop, one of the participants asked: "Should I use one or the other technique or can I combine the two together?"

I said *it depends*.

Allow me to explain. Sure, all of the interventions in this chapter have been shown to work in experimental trials. But you still may find some more useful than others.

The analogy I use is that it's like deciding what pill to pop to treat a headache. Some people swear by ibuprofen. Others prefer good old paracetamol. A few will stick with aspirin. And there are those who crave the double whammy of paracetamol mixed with codeine.

I suggest that you test-drive the assorted techniques to see what works best for you. Think of it as your own series of experiments. Keep trying different things and reviewing the results until you find the ones that feel the most comfortable and effective for you.

You may find that writing power paragraphs gives you the lift you need while re-reading about the illusion of transparency leaves you cold – or vice versa. You may discover that telling yourself "I'm excited" helps during a big presentation, job interview, date or whatever. But you will only discover such lessons by *trying* all of the techniques, actually putting them into practice on multiple occasions.

Consider also how a shot of confidence will help those around you to make an impact. If you're one of the lucky few for whom self-confidence isn't an issue, think about spreading the message. Whether it's friends who need more social confidence or fellows at work who could do with being more assertive, what mental manoeuvres could be of benefit to them?

Onwards and upwards

- Understand that being in the right mental state can make an absolutely real difference to your performance, your standing, your persuasiveness. Whether you're dealing with one person, many or – heck – even someone reading a written application, there are proven techniques that can combat anxiety and help you to stand out for the right reasons.
- Remember the confidence con: other people may outwardly appear confident, but you can't know how worried or intimidated they may feel inwardly. So don't believe for one moment that you're the only person in the world who ever feels panicky or lacking in confidence. There are probably large numbers of people around you right now who appear confident but who don't feel confident at all.
- Bear in mind also the illusion of transparency. Just because you are so aware of your own physical nervousness – the racing heart, sweaty palms, the worrisome thoughts swirling in your head – doesn't mean others can see it. Simply reminding yourself of this illusion of transparency can help you appear more credible and eloquent to others.
- Remember that you will get the benefit from *applying* the techniques, not merely understanding them. Several of them require putting pen to paper because that is the proven way to get benefits. Don't make the mistake that simply reading the chapter will give you the swashbuckling confidence you seek.
- In your quest to stand out, test the different techniques within this chapter and see what works best for you. If one technique feels clunky for you personally, try something else. Have a go at marrying different ones together to see what gives you the biggest lift.

2

Persuading through Body Language and Nonverbal Communication

The medium is the message.
Marshall McLuhan

You've probably sat through a fair number of boring speeches and presentations. But I'd argue that it's not just the content – what's being said – that can switch you off. The best speakers and presenters have a certain manner, a way of being and behaving, that makes you sit up and take notice.

Flash back to June. I was sitting with 50 or so business professionals in an audience waiting for a seminar to begin on the topic of innovation at work. Bright morning sunshine streamed through floor-to-ceiling windows and there was an eager buzz of expectation in the air. The agenda informed us that there were two speakers. One of them I'll call Thomas Gray. The other was Monica Parker, a director at office design consultancy Morgan Lovell.

First up was Gray. Wearing a subtly patterned grey shirt and grey-brown jumper, he stood up to speak. He introduced himself and talked about the business that he represented, a firm with tens of thousands of employees worldwide.

I was only sitting in the second row but I couldn't quite catch everything he said. But within minutes it became apparent that other people were also struggling to hear him as an enterprising assistant glided over to hand him a microphone.

His voice boomed out of twin speakers on either side of the room. Marvellous. We could hear him at least.

It took me just another minute to notice that he spent around two-thirds of his time looking at the projection of his slides behind him. He spent the other third of the time looking at only a sliver of his audience – the people on his far most right side. I was on his left so didn't get even a moment of eye contact from him during the entirety of his 15-minute presentation.

He pretty much remained rooted to the spot. His left leg stayed planted on the floor and he rocked only very slowly back and forth. One moment his weight was over his left foot. Ten seconds later, it was over his right foot. Another dozen seconds later, it was back over the left. A gentle, soporific shift. And when he did walk around, he did so timidly. He didn't move so much as sag from one position to the next.

Neither was Gray someone who gestured a lot. His left arm remained mainly down by his side. His right arm, he occasionally lifted to point to his slides.

The thing is: his topic was actually pretty interesting. Working for a big brand you'd know, an international technology company, he talked about the rapid pace of change in the world. He cited as evidence the fact that photography business Eastman Kodak and technology firm Palm (creator of 1990s must-have device the Palm Pilot, arguably the forerunner to the iPhone) were once stock market darlings, proud members of the Standard & Poor's 500 and amongst some of the world's most valued companies. Where are they now? Gone. Dust. Footnotes in history.

The best speakers and presenters have a certain manner, a way of being and behaving, that makes you sit up and take notice.

Not wanting to get left behind, his organization was racing to launch new products and lines of business. He described his role in helping his business to become more agile and quicker to market. The pace of innovation in the world means that large companies simply can't rest on their laurels. They need to innovate or die. It really is that stark.

Gray's message was compelling. His candid description of his company's efforts to stay relevant was fascinating too – or it *should* have been. But unfortunately he looked and sounded slightly disconnected from the topic. Scanning the room, I noticed a handful of individuals checking their phones. Whether they were responding to crucial emails or playing Candy Crush, I couldn't tell.

He received a smattering of applause and then it was Monica Parker's turn.

As workplace director of her business, Parker was responsible for promoting the firm's office design capabilities. So we in the audience were expecting to hear how working patterns are changing, how technology can improve office productivity and how employees' needs for privacy can be balanced against bosses' desires to cut costs and move everybody to open-plan arrangements.

A statuesque figure in a cranberry-coloured shift dress topped with a short, sharp bob of dark hair and equally sharp cheekbones, she took hold of the microphone but covered it with her other hand. In a clear, loud voice, she asked the audience, "I'm not used to needing a microphone. Do I need it?"

Several dozen people in the audience shook their heads. A couple of us – including me – said no.

So immediately she jolted the audience into paying attention. Her voice was demonstrably louder than Gray's. And the fact that her voice emanated from her – as opposed to speakers on either side of the audience – made it easier for us to connect with her.

"I'm really *struck* about the *nature* of change and the *speed* of change that we're experiencing these days," she told us, emphasizing key words. Her eyes swung from left to right and back again, encompassing the whole audience in her gaze.

"I thought I'd talk a little bit about what innovation at work *is* and, more importantly, what it *isn't*."

Her voice was full of intonation. She stressed words and used pitch, varying the speed and tone of her delivery from one sentence to the next. She spoke quickly most of the time but paused occasionally and lingeringly for dramatic effect. She had the kind of speaking voice that could make the phonebook sound entertaining.

Parker talked through a handful of slides but the audience's focus was squarely on her. Apart from being louder, she spoke much more quickly than Gray too. The words tumbled out of her at literally twice the rate of Gray's.

She had her projected slides to her right but she was moving, constantly moving. She held her elbows away from her body and she pointed, gestured with her palms up, balled her hands into fists at times. She stepped from side to side, sometimes back and forth. I pressed the stopwatch button on my watch and timed her: she paced or shifted her weight 35 times in a single minute.

And she looked at the audience. Looking to her left, looking to the right. Glanced at people in the front occasionally but also included the handful of folks that couldn't get seats and who stood at the back. She flashed her eyes. She smiled and laughed but composed her face to cover more sombre verdicts too.

Like Gray, she also spoke for around 15 minutes, but what Parker gave was not a mere speech or presentation. It was a *performance.*

When she finished, I clapped effusively. And I found myself smiling. I couldn't help it. I found it pretty *thrilling*, which isn't a word I use lightly. I'm a tough critic and not easily impressed.

Afterwards, I chatted to some of the other members of the audience. As we tucked into miniature bacon sandwiches, a laidback New Zealander admitted that he couldn't remember the name of the first presenter. John? Richard? Carl?

"I really enjoyed Monica's presentation, though," he added.

Now the differences between the two presentations may have been down to many reasons. Perhaps Gray had less time to prepare. He probably presented less frequently than Parker. But for whatever reason, Parker made an impact while Gray did not.

Parker had clearly honed her craft. And research tells us that presenting well is a craft as opposed to an innate talent. Personally, I've worked with people who have gone from being merely competent to fairly impressive presenters as well as individuals who have gone from forgettable to capable.

Presenting well is a craft as opposed to an innate talent. Presenting at work, giving a speech at a wedding, pitching a product from a tradeshow booth, making yourself appear interesting at a party or at a networking meeting. These are all opportunities to stand out and get your message across. So how do body language and nonverbal communication help us deliver the punchiest calls to action possible?

Understanding your nonverbal style

Parker is an elegant example of someone who uses nonverbal communication very fruitfully. But before we delve too much further into the science of nonverbal communication, here's a chance for you to learn something about how you measure up. Take a look at the following statements. If you'd like to learn a little more about yourself, please rate the extent to which you agree or disagree with each statement on the five-point scale indicated.

If you prefer, you can also take the questionnaire online by visiting my website:

www.robyeung.com/howtostandout

You will need to enter the password for the page: #howtostandout#

	1 – disagree strongly	2 – disagree	3 – neither agree nor disagree	4 – agree	5 – agree strongly
1. When I hear good dance music, I can hardly keep still.					
2. I can easily express emotion over the telephone.					
3. I often touch friends during conversations.					
4. My laugh is soft and subdued.					
5. I dislike being watched by a large group of people.					
6. I usually have a neutral facial expression.					
7. I like to remain unnoticed in a crowd.					
8. I am shy among strangers.					
9. I am terrible at pantomime as in games like charades.					

(*Continued*)

53

	1 – disagree strongly	2 – disagree	3 – neither agree nor disagree	4 – agree	5 – agree strongly
10. People tell me that I would make a good actor or actress.					
11. I am able to give a seductive glance if I want to.					
12. At small parties, I am the centre of attention.					
13. I show that I like someone by hugging or touching that person.					

To work out your overall nonverbal expressiveness, begin by adding up the scores you got for statements 1, 2, 3, 10, 11, 12 and 13. Write that score down first. That gives you an Expressive Communication score of between 7 and 35.

Next, for statements 4 to 9, subtract the score you gave yourself in each instance from the number 6. For instance, if you ticked the box "2 – disagree" for one of these statements, then you take 2 away from 6, which gives you 4. Add up the reversed scores for statements 4 to 9 to give you an Inward Communication score of between 6 and 30.

Finally, add up your Expressive Communication and Inward Communication scores together to give you an overall score of between

13 and 65. Remember, however, that if you find reversing the scores and adding everything up manually to be too much hassle, you can visit the webpage www.robyeung.com/howtostandout – remember to pop in the password #howtostandout#.

You've probably completed online quizzes or questionnaires in magazines such as *Cosmopolitan* or *Men's Health*. The problem with most tests is that they have been dreamed up by hacks or purported experts with no scientific testing; there's no evidence that they actually predict people's behaviour or performance. They may be fun but they are no more rigorous than a questionnaire that you or one of your friends might make up for a laugh; they won't teach you anything truly insightful about yourself.

This questionnaire is different. It's a true psychometric test. The 13 statements come from the minds of psychology professor Howard Friedman and his compatriots at University of California, Riverside. Even though it's a self-report test – i.e. one in which we rate ourselves as to how we think we behave – it has actually been demonstrated to be a fairly robust measure of how nonverbally expressive others see us.

High scorers tend to have had theatrical experience – either having performed professionally or in amateur troupes. High scorers are also more likely to have had political experience, of having been elected into an official role. High scorers also tend to be overrepresented in the selling profession, where persuasion and being an electrifying communicator are indispensable skills.[1]

In addition, Friedman and his associates found that American physicians who scored higher on the test tended to have more patients. Remember that healthcare in the United States is not free. Patients have to pay to visit doctors so they are much more discerning in their choice of whether to leave or stick with a doctor than in many European countries, where healthcare may be free or heavily subsidized by the government.

Taking all of these pieces of evidence together, Friedman and his team concluded that the questionnaire can be used as a rough measure of nonverbal expressiveness. Putting it another way, the test is a measure of communication *interestingness*. How animated, engaging and frankly entertaining are you when you speak?

Your score	Interpretation
31	90 per cent of people score higher than you
37	75 per cent of people score higher than you
42	You are exactly at the midpoint on the test, making you statistically average
47	You score higher than 75 per cent of people
50	You score higher than 90 per cent of people

The test was originally devised in 1980. So, to ensure that it still stands up to scrutiny in the fast-paced contemporary world, I set out to check whether it could still distinguish between highly expressive and less expressive individuals. I administered the test to several hundred people and created the data table above. So you can rest assured that the questionnaire measures relative expressiveness in modern times rather than a bygone age.

How animated, engaging and frankly entertaining are you when you speak?

Lower scores (i.e. lower than the midpoint of 42) suggest you are nonverbally less expressive than most people. So you may be someone who speaks more quietly, perhaps more reservedly, than others. You may not always enjoy drawing attention to yourself; you may often get as much out of simply being with others and enjoying their company as being the star of the show. You probably feel somewhat less comfortable using your hands to gesticulate too wildly or allowing the canvas of your face to reveal too vividly how you're really feeling.

High scores imply greater levels of nonverbal expressiveness. So you probably speak fairly loudly or you use a lot of variation in the volume of your voice. You don't mind being the centre of attention; you may even revel in the spotlight. Friends and colleagues may describe you as being quite vivacious or even dramatic in your behaviour, for example when you're telling stories about what you've been up to. You're probably also the kind of person who lifts your eyebrows, smiles and frowns, laughs and gasps to portray your emotions. The higher your score above 42, the more this description is likely to apply to you.

Just as a point of comparison, Monica Parker scored 55 on the test. That puts her in the top 1 per cent of the population. But the test merely confirms what I saw with my own eyes: that she was a vibrant, entertaining, standout individual.

Understanding the power of what's not said

Of course, being memorable and persuasive involves many factors. For example, we all know that physically attractive people tend to do better in life. We're more likely to take notice of individuals we find attractive than those we find less attractive.

But a mountain of studies suggest that, all other things being equal, people who are more nonverbally expressive may do better in life. In a follow-up study, for example, Howard Friedman's crew asked 54 undergraduate students to fill in a battery of personality tests including the test of nonverbal expressiveness that you've already seen in this chapter. The researchers then planted hidden cameras in a laboratory before asking the students to enter the laboratory one at a time to meet a group of strangers.

People who are more nonverbally expressive may do better in life.

When Friedman and co later played back the video clips to other observers, they unsurprisingly found that physically attractive individuals tended to be rated as more likeable than those who were less physically attractive. Duh. That's what's known as a no-brainer, right?

However, the investigators also found a separate effect: those folks who were more nonverbally expressive were also rated as more likeable. Putting it another way, expressiveness helped people to get noticed – irrespective of how physically attractive or unattractive they were.[2]

Now you may wonder how being more likeable helps us. But think about all of the celebrities who are paid to endorse products: Hollywood actors, TV presenters, sports personalities. Why? Because more than any other single quality, we trust people we like.

But nonverbal expressiveness doesn't just help people to become more likeable. Other evidence suggests that nonverbal expressiveness is linked to a person's overall attractiveness, their allure and outright sexiness too.

More than any other single quality, we trust people we like. In a classic study, social science investigators Ronald Sabatelli and Michal Rubin looked at the link between nonverbal expressiveness and attractiveness by luring intrepid participants – 15 men and 15 women – to allow themselves to be judged by others on not only their physical appearance but also their nonverbal expressiveness. Again, the men and women who were more nonverbally expressive – i.e. those who used more spontaneous, uncensored nonverbal behaviour – tended to be rated as more attractive than those who were more buttoned-up.[3]

So, yes, a big chunk of sexual attractiveness is about the curve of your nose, the symmetry of your face, the shape of your body and the many other cues that media and culture feed us. But there's also something else that comes down not to the contours or size of your body but the way you use it, the way you move, the way you *are*.

I am happy to accept that nonverbally expressive people may be more sexually alluring. That's not a big deal. It doesn't matter too much in the grand scheme of things. But should we allow more expressive people to win us over on the really important decisions in life too?

Take the decision about who should be running the country, for instance. When it comes to election time, how do you decide which politician to support? Erik Bucy, a professor of communication studies at Texas Tech University, published a paper looking at the link between US presidential candidates' nonverbal behaviour and the extent to which the public wanted to vote for them.

By analysing people's Twitter comments in real time in response to televised presidential debates, he concluded that people were far more swayed by politicians' gestures, facial expressions and tone of voice than what they actually said.[4] Bucy wrote: "People respond a lot to behaviour. Not everybody pays really that close of attention to elections or knows all their party's positions on the issues, but they can get a sense of the candidates' traits by observing [their nonverbal] behaviour."[5]

I find it somewhat scary that we are all inveigled by nonverbal tactics even when it comes to such major decisions. But all of these pieces of evidence point to a single conclusion: people are often less influenced by what you say than how you say it. Nonverbal communication *matters*.

People are often less influenced by what you say than how you say it.

59

Understanding the three nonverbal communication tactics

How often do you gesture or point with your hands when you speak? Do you lean forwards or sit back? When presenting, do you stand still behind a lectern or move around the room? Is your voice loud and booming, a quiet whisper or one that alternates between the two?

All of these are facets of nonverbal communication. Nonverbal cues essentially cover everything apart from the words themselves – from our facial expressions, gestures and movements to the tone of our voices and the pauses we use in our speech.

A low score on the nonverbal expressiveness test suggests you deploy nonverbal cues in a more restrained fashion. A high score suggests you are a lot more animated and energetic in their use.

Most psychologists break nonverbal cues into three broad categories:

- **Facial expressions.** These include everything you do with your face, from smiling when you're amused to scrunching up your nose and narrowing your eyes when you feel disgusted.
- **Gestures and bodily movement.** These include everything from the way we shake, nod and tilt our heads to our use of posture and the ways we gesticulate with our hands.
- **Vocal prosody.** This final category describes the rhythm, loudness, stress and intonation of speech – i.e. everything about the voice apart from the words themselves.

When we discussed the nonverbal expressiveness questionnaire, you may have come to the conclusion that more nonverbal behaviour is generally better. And that's mostly true.

But it's also a slight oversimplification. So let's examine more in-depth studies to see exactly how each of these three categories can contribute to making us more enthralling and charismatic.

Painting on the canvas of the human face

Early studies looking at how people used nonverbal behaviour to make an impact tended to look at what specific movements and facial expressions meant. So nodding the head is a fairly universal sign – at least in Western culture – for acceptance of what's being said. Similarly, balling the fingers of the hand into a fist but allowing the thumb to stick up is an Anglo-American sign that things are going well.

Can you recognize what particular nonverbal signals are supposed to mean? In 2011, a squad of researchers led by Elisabeth André at the University of Augsburg in Germany published a paper comprehensively reviewing the meanings of different nonverbal cues. Of particular interest was a table drawn up by the scientists that alleged to identify the meanings of certain common cues involving either the head or a facial expression – or in some cases the two together.[6]

Researchers that have shown video clips of the nonverbal cues on the left-hand side of the table have typically found that most Western European observers come to similar conclusions about the meaning of each behaviour. How many of them can you interpret correctly in the table below? I'll start you off with two of the easiest ones. And I'll put the completed table with all of the supposed meanings at the end of this chapter.

Nonverbal cue	Meaning
Head nod	Acceptance of what's being said or done
Head nod + smile	
Tilt head to side + sad eyebrows	
Eye roll	
Tilt head to side + gaze down	
Shake head + frown + tense lips	
Head shake	Rejection of what's being said or done
Head shake + frown	
Tilt head to side + frown	
Eyes wide open	

Did you have a go at trying to suss out what each combination of head movement and expression was supposed to mean? Now, perhaps your reaction was similar to mine when I first saw the list. The meanings may be right, but I'm not sure how useful they actually are. Sure, these cues may allow you to communicate disagreement or liking. But that seems to be just about it. They don't exactly give us much of a repertoire to use across lots of different situations. Indeed, studies have not shown that teaching people the individual nonverbal cues in that table actually help them to become more persuasive.

My advice? Don't worry about trying to master individual facial expressions and head movements. Rather than deconstructing individual nonverbal cues, we'll see later on that it may be more profitable to think about the whole.

Becoming pitch perfect

The previous table looked only at the interplay between head movements and facial expressions. And in an ideal world, we would be able to put together a list of behaviours covering every permutation of facial expressions, gestures and vocal qualities to allow us to achieve different effects. Alas, that often isn't possible.

It's not merely that such a table would get devilishly complicated. Instead, researchers have found that not all nonverbal gestures are equally helpful in all situations.

Let's take the example of how we use our voices, for starters. If we look at one study on the pitch of a speaker's voice, it seems to paint a fairly clear picture – at least at first.

To set the scene, think about the politicians you admire. Yes, I know you probably don't admire many politicians. So you may have to think long and hard.

Ask a group of people why they vote for one politician over another and you may hear them mention factors such as their policies, experience, likeability, personality, leadership qualities and trustworthiness. We saw earlier in the chapter from Erik Bucy's analysis of Twitter users that the masses were indeed influenced by politicians' nonverbal cues. But to what extent did just the sound of their voices make a difference?

Not all nonverbal gestures are equally helpful in all situations.

University of Miami political scientist Casey Klofstad wanted hard data to prove or disprove the importance of voice for once and for all. So he clubbed together with Duke University biologists Rindy Anderson and Susan Peters to record men and women saying a single sentence: "I urge you to vote for me this November."

Playing pairs of higher- versus lower-pitched men's voices to listeners, they found that both male and female listeners said they would rather vote for the lower-pitched candidate. Now, the fact that audiences prefer deeper voices in men should hardly come as a shock. Men with deeper voices tend to be larger and physically hardier. So a deeper voice is like an evolutionary signal for brute strength and a man's survival and reproductive fitness.[7]

Perhaps more interestingly, though, both male and female listeners also preferred the deeper woman's voice. In fact, when the architects of the study delved further into the issue and asked listeners to rate the character of each candidate, they found that "higher-pitched female voices are judged to be weaker, less competent and less trustworthy". Ouch.

As an aside, remember that this isn't *my* opinion. I, Rob Yeung, am not personally criticizing women with higher-pitched voices. This is simply what the science tells us. Deeper voices are perceived as more leader-like, strong and competent in both men and women. So if your aim is to be seen this way, you may want to train yourself to speak in the lower part of your register.

Deeper voices are perceived as more leader-like, strong and competent.

Okay. That's straightforward enough so far. However, when we look at the relationship between vocal pitch and impact outside of the workplace, things get muddier.

For men's voices, the picture remains fairly clear. Several studies conducted in different countries around the world have found that women typically find lower-pitched male voices more attractive. Women listeners also tend to judge deeper voices as being both more masculine and healthier too – again evidence that a deeper male voice is an evolutionary signal for a high-quality, healthy mate.[8]

Taking these results into account, we can conclude that men with lower voices tend to be perceived not only as more leader-like but also as more attractive – more suitable as a potential mate. So if you're a single guy on the lookout for love, you may wish to pay attention. Get growling: *grrrr*.

However, studies tell us that men tend to find *higher* pitches in women more attractive. Men judge higher-pitched female voices to be more feminine, younger and healthier.[9]

So while Casey Klofstad and his partners found that a lower-pitched woman's voice makes her sound more leader-like in the workplace, it may actually be less sexually attractive to men. Saying that a woman has a *girly* voice may be considered an insult in the office but a compliment in a bar or nightclub. Unluckily for women, what helps at work may not help at play.

> **Men tend to find *higher* pitches in women more attractive.**

Choosing the right speaking velocity

The research on pitch isn't exactly helpful – at least for women. Do studies enlighten us further about other vocal characteristics?

Consider the relationship between people's loudness and their impact, for example. A 2015 study led by San Diego State University psychologist Sei Jin Ko found that audiences tended to rate louder speakers as being significantly more powerful than quieter individuals. But that's hardly news – it's what we've known all along. Speak quietly and you get described as mousy, shy and forgettable. Speak up and immediately everybody thinks you're more powerful and impressive.

> **Speak up and immediately everybody thinks you're more powerful and impressive.**

But perhaps lessons about the *speed* with which we speak may turn out to be more counterintuitive.

The English actor Sir Michael Caine once remarked: "The basic rule of human nature is that powerful people speak slowly and subservient people quickly, because if they don't speak fast nobody will listen to them."

It's a popular quote that has been repeated on dozens of websites, in magazines and books too. The line is often used by trainers who teach public speaking skills to indicate that we should all speak more slowly. For example, one website I found claimed that speaking more slowly "gives the subliminal message that you are important". Other authors have suggested that speaking too quickly reduces comprehension: that it's harder for audiences to grasp a message when the words are being fired at them. Heck, *I* once used the quote in a book (quite a few years ago) to suggest that we should all speak more slowly.

But is it really the case that speaking more slowly makes us appear more convincing and worthier of attention?

Contemplate for a moment how you would run an experiment to evaluate the effects of speech rate on persuasion and credibility. One method might be to record the same message at different speeds, play them to various listeners and ask them to rate which they find more persuasive and credible.

And that's pretty much what psychologist Norman Miller and his associates at the University of Southern California did. They recorded three versions of the same statements to play to passers-by in a local shopping mall. His research assistants approached strangers in the shopping centre and introduced themselves as correspondents from radio station KSC interviewing people on the street for a programme called *People's Forum*. The unknowing participants in the experiment were asked to listen to a short recording of around 300 words in length describing the alleged dangers of hydroponically grown vegetables.

According to the recording, growing vegetables in hydroponic gardens – i.e. cultivating them in nutrient solutions rather than soil – was associated with a raft of problems. The voice on the recording claimed that frequent tests were necessary to ensure the right chemical concentrations in the growing solution. And it could cause cellular defects and genetic abnormalities in the crops too. Scary stuff – at least allegedly.

Listeners were played the same message but delivered at one of three different speeds: 111, 140 or 191 words per minute. Immediately afterwards, they were asked to rate their agreement with the argument that hydroponic methods were dangerous; they were also asked to judge the speaker's intelligence, knowledge and objectivity too.

So what do you reckon? Would slow or fast – or somewhere in between – get the best reactions from listeners?

The results found a clear benefit for quicker speech rates. Far from losing listeners or bewildering them, the fastest rate scored better on every outcome. The quickest speaker was judged to be persuasive, more intelligent, as having greater knowledge and being more objective.[10]

Neither was Miller's study a fluke result. Another piece of research conducted jointly by scientists William Apple and Robert Krauss from Columbia University, and Lynn Streeter at the private research outfit Bell Laboratories, concluded: "Slow-talking speakers were judged less truthful, less fluent, and less persuasive." They were also considered slower, colder, more passive and weaker than speedier speakers.[11] Ouch.

So it seems that speaking more quickly – like Monica Parker at the workplace innovation seminar – is associated with a raft of benefits. Sadly, English thespian Michael Caine appears to have been

Speaking more quickly is associated with a raft of benefits.

incorrect about the connection between slower speech and power. As a result, *I* was wrong to use that quote all those years ago to imply that slower speech was a good thing.

Thinking about Caine's quote, I think it's probably more likely that powerful people can speak however the hell they like – slow, fast, with a funny accent or in whatever manner they choose – because others simply have to put up with it. But for most of us, speaking a little more quickly may actually help to convey a greater sense of dynamism as well as being more persuasive.

Injecting energy into speeches and conversations

The fact that high-speed speakers are rated as more truthful, fluent and persuasive than slower speakers doesn't mean you should merely aim to spit your words out more quickly and loudly. No. That could lead to disaster.

When I'm training people in giving more effective, more compelling presentations, I recommend they first practise what they want to say. Because the more you practise, the more familiar you will become with your content. And when you feel more comfortable with the words you wish to deliver, *that's* when you can play around with vocal prosody – the rhythm and pacing of what you want to say.

So please don't take these studies as a recommendation that you should blurt everything out more quickly regardless of the situation. No. Instead, think about spending a little more time practising for those big occasions – whether it's a key presentation or an important date. Familiarize yourself with your material first and *only then* ratchet up your speech rate.

Indicating intent through gestures and animation

We move now to arguably the most challenging and complex area of nonverbal communication: the dance involving our arms and legs, our postures, our eight fingers and two thumbs.

A few months before I sat down to write the first draft of this chapter, I attended a seminar run by BCMS, a consultancy offering advice to business owners looking to sell their businesses. The lead presenter, David Rebbettes, helped to found the business in 1989 and had spent a considerable portion of the subsequent decades travelling both nationally and internationally as a spokesperson for the company. In other words, he had spoken to live audiences on hundreds if not thousands of occasions.

Rebbettes, a somewhat hulking man with a bald head and manicured goatee, approached the low mobile lectern set up at the front of the room. Clad in a discreet corporate uniform of a dark suit and striped tie, he never moved from behind the lectern. He kept his feet planted solidly behind the lectern for the entirety of his presentation.

To begin with, he seemed a little nervous. He spent a considerable part of the first minute or two wringing his hands together. But after those moments of seeming nervousness, he relaxed and became a rather compelling speaker.

Even though his feet remained firmly planted in place, his hands and, in fact, whole upper body compensated by remaining ceaselessly in motion. He did occasionally rest his hands on the hip-height lectern, but this was often so that he could dip his shoulders forward and lean in towards the audience. Lowering his voice to a stage whisper, his eyes darted left and right as if he were letting the audience in on secrets that only they were privy to.

At one point he talked through how BCMS had observed that the prices buyers were willing to pay could vary considerably. "The difference between the highest offer and the lowest offer is consistently two and a half times," he said. Simultaneously, he raised his right hand above his head, with the palm facing down to punctuate the word "highest". And then he dropped his hand to belly height to indicate the "lowest" offer.

"Can I give you some examples? We've got hundreds upon hundreds upon hundreds of examples of companies we've sold." Every time he said the word "hundreds", he pushed his upturned hands wider and wider away from his body, as if to illustrate that he had so many examples that he couldn't keep hold of them physically.

As an example, he talked about a travel business that had been bought for a very high price by the online travel giant Expedia. Why was Expedia willing to pay such a premium? "Expedia could grow the company further than any of the other bidders. Expedia could grow this company quicker than any of the other bidders. And Expedia was willing to outbid any of the other bidders." Each time Rebbettes mentioned one of the reasons Expedia had bought the business, he counted a point off on his fingers, starting with the fifth finger of his left hand, then the fourth, then the middle finger.

I typically think of movement around the room as a good thing for presenters. It adds to the feeling of dynamism, that a presentation or speech has momentum and is going somewhere. But Rebbettes proved me wrong.

It isn't necessary to walk around a room so long as a presenter exploits other nonverbal cues. And this was certainly true for Rebbettes, who used not only his hands but also his entire arm.

He often spread his arms wider than his shoulders to emphasize the monumental opportunities available to us in the audience. At times, he flung his hands above his head. Every so often, he clasped his hands together in exhortation. In other words, he gave his presentation as much through his hands as through his words. It was like sign language for hearing folks. If nothing else, using gestures makes a presenter visually entertaining.

If nothing else, using gestures makes a presenter visually entertaining.

Now, Rebbettes may be a beautiful example of how gestures help us to stand out and hold sway over others. But then again, he could just be an exception, an outlier. In order to look at the importance of gestures for the rest of us, we need to turn to scientific inquiry. Do gestures, posture and physical animation genuinely make a difference in the high-pressure world of pitching and selling?

To answer the question, sales management gurus Thomas Leigh at the University of Georgia and John Summers at Indiana University recorded videos of salespeople's pitches. Some of the videos showed sales executives dipping and bouncing with physical animation; others were notably more reserved.

The researchers then recruited 90 professional buyers to watch the recorded sales presentations. Leigh and Summers predicted that the livelier sellers would reap more positive reviews.

But they were wrong. The buyers were not influenced by the extent to which a salesperson either slumped in his seat or sat upright with a rigidly straight back. Neither were the buyers influenced by a salesperson's use of gestures. More gesticulation with the hands led to no more impact than little or no gesturing.[12]

I fancy that the sales management researchers may have felt somewhat deflated. After all, they had set out to verify that gestures mattered. That more emphatic utilization of the hands helps salespeople to be more impactful and convincing. But that was categorically not the case. So if *more* gestures don't help us to be more influential, what does?

Delving deeper into gestures

To unravel the conundrum of gestures and their effects on people, allow me to introduce you to social scientist Fridanna Maricchiolo. But be glad that you're only reading about her because you would no doubt be extremely self-conscious about your hand gestures if you were ever to meet her. Having won the national Italian Association of Psychology top prize for her 2005 doctoral dissertation on the relationship between hand gestures and persuasion, she is fast being recognized as an international authority on the true impact of nonverbal behaviour.

Maricchiolo, an assistant professor of psychology at the University of Roma Tre in Italy, wondered whether it was not the *extent* to which we gesture but the *type* of gesture we use that affects how we are perceived by others. Based on her observations of people's natural behaviour, she has divided hand gestures into four broad categories.[13]

Let's take our time to look at them in detail. Here are the first two:

- **Ideational gestures** tend to reinforce the meaning of what's being said. For example, a friend retelling how he knocked over a cup of coffee during a date might sweep his elbow sideways to demonstrate the motion. A manager allocating tasks to members of the team might point to different individuals. Ideational gestures also include symbolic gestures that everybody in a given culture tends to understand, such as the thumbs-up gesture to represent 'OK' or raising a middle finger as a sign of anger or hatred. Or a salesperson emphasizing his honesty might shrug and offer up the palms of both hands.

72

- **Conversational gestures** are hand or finger movements that accompany speech but may be either planned or unplanned. Many people wave their hands around in an apparently erratic fashion when speaking. These gestures may not be intended to communicate a message in the same way as ideational gestures; however, conversational gestures often seem to fit with the general message. So a friend speaking about how he was rushing around might move his arms around more frantically; a colleague confessing to a major mistake might move very little or not at all.

Maricchiolo also separated out another two categories of so-called adaptor gestures, which are movements with our hands or bodies we may make in response to the situations we're in. Many researchers believe these may be in adaptation – hence the name – to being in, say, a stressful or particularly exciting situation. There are two categories of adaptor gestures:

- **Object-adaptor gestures** are movements that involve external objects. For example, drumming your fingers on a desk, playing with a pen or repeatedly touching your jewellery could signal anything from boredom or impatience to anxiety and consternation. A smoker waving a cigarette around during conversation or a presenter twiddling a marker pen in front of a whiteboard would be said to be making object-adaptor gestures too.
- **Self-adaptor gestures** are movements or touches that involve ourselves. So stroking your chin, twirling a lock of hair, crossing your legs, hugging your arms across your body and any other actions that involve contact of your own body parts with other parts of yourself would all be considered self-adaptors.

In order to inspect the statistical relationships between different gestures and their impact, Maricchiolo's team asked groups of up to eight people at a time to engage in video-recorded debates for around 40 minutes at a time. At the end of each discussion, she asked each participant to fill in a questionnaire to rate the credibility and impact of everyone else in the group.

Next came the analysis. When the researchers played back the video recordings and timed how long each participant spoke, they quickly spotted a blueprint for standing out. Participants who spoke more tended to be judged by everybody else as more dominant and influential than those who spoke less.

It's a somewhat dispiriting finding but one that probably echoes what you have likely always suspected: the more loquacious amongst us – those who spend the most time talking – tend to get noticed. No matter how extraordinary the quality of your thinking, no one can acknowledge it unless you speak out.

No matter how extraordinary the quality of your thinking, no one can acknowledge it unless you speak out.

But that was an almost tangential finding. Remember that Maricchiolo and her colleagues were most interested in how different gestures may help or hamper us. And when the investigative team analysed the types of gesture that each participant exhibited, they found an intriguing pattern of results. When participants spoke less, they were generally rated by their fellow debaters as being less influential *unless* those participants used more gestures.

But not all gestures were equally helpful. Only participants who employed a lot of ideational, conversational and/or object-adaptor gestures managed to increase their impact despite having said less. Participants who used more self-adaptor gestures did not get any benefit.[14]

There's quite a lot of jargon here about the different types of gesture. So let's try to review the study's findings in plain English. Essentially, people who talk a lot tend to get a lot of attention and glory in meetings. Whether they use their hands frequently or hardly at all doesn't make a great deal of difference because they are taking up so much air time anyway.

However, people who talk less can still command attention by using their hands more – by illustrating the concepts they're discussing and demonstrating the actions they propose. So this suggests that those of us who are less comfortable filling the conversational space with words can maximize our impact by using our hands more when we do speak.

Going back to the earlier inquiry by Leigh and Summers on gestures and salesperson effectiveness, we can perhaps guess why gestures didn't make a difference. Their sales executives may have been so gifted or seasoned that their words alone were enough to make an impact.

People who talk less can still command attention by using their hands more.

Gestures aren't always necessary, then. If you have a compelling argument and speak in a determined and vigorous fashion, you'll make a big impact. But even if you are more hesitant or reserved in what you say, you can make a more stalwart impression by reinforcing your message in how you say it – especially with your hands.

Giving yourself a gestural advantage

The study by Maricchiolo and her colleagues suggests that gestures are of most benefit to those who are more reticent in making their case and pushing for air time. If you're certain that your words are so compelling, so profound or even momentous that people simply must sit up and take notice, by all means ignore your hands.

But if you need to make more of an impact, gesture more. Think of communication as theatre, a mingling of not only words but also performance.

Remember, though, that it's not just about gesturing more. The *type* of gesture we use matters. Only three of the four categories

(Continued)

of gesture helped more introverted individuals boost their impact. If you yearn to be seen as more charismatic, mull over how you might integrate more of the following into your repertoire:

- **Ideational gestures.** Think about the illustrative or symbolic gestures you use. How would you indicate a concept such as width? You might spread your hands apart with palms facing each other. Height? You may lift one hand with your palm facing down. Or consider the gestures you might employ to illustrate concepts or actions such as "circle", "snake", "turn the volume up" or "bring two groups together".
- **Conversational gestures.** Watch politicians emphasizing their points on television and you'll often see them slashing, waving or pointing with their hands. For example, imagine someone saying the sentence, "We will not, I repeat, not back down on this point." You can easily see how the word "not" could be emphasized both times with a brandished fist or a Kung Fu-like chop, for example. That may not make a great deal of sense in print, but watch people on television with a more analytical eye and you'll see what I'm getting at.
- **Object-adaptors.** Clearly, fidgeting with an object such as a pen or your phone gives rise to the wrong kind of impression. But tapping a table or jabbing a lectern at times could again be used to emphasize key words.

Remember that the last category of gestures was the self-adaptors. These by definition involve touching our own body parts with other parts of our body. And many of these gestures – such as crossing our arms across our body, playing with our hair, wringing our hands, touching our faces or scratching ourselves – are commonly seen as signifying anxiety or deception. So perhaps it's no surprise that self-adaptor gestures had little effect on perceived influence.

The clear lesson: by all means draw upon your hands to signal your dynamism. But keep your hands away from your body.

Combining nonverbal cues

So far we've examined the components of body language and non-verbal communication piece by piece. So we've looked at head nods and facial expressions, speed of speech and vocal pitch as well as various gestures. Clearly, becoming more influential nonverbally isn't about using these elements one at a time. It's about blending them together.

In the quest to scrutinize nonverbal cues together rather than in isolation, competing groups of researchers have invented different coding schemes to gauge the extent to which speakers come across as charismatic. One of the best of these measurement methods was developed in the early 1990s but continues to be used today.

Consider a study in which British academics Timothy Clark and David Greatbatch at Durham Business School analysed videos of speeches given by individuals widely regarded as influential thought leaders. The subjects under scrutiny included *The 7 Habits of Highly Effective People* author Stephen Covey, management guru Tom Peters, emotional intelligence writer Daniel Goleman and Harvard Business School professor Rosabeth Moss Kanter.[15]

The researchers began by asking an audience of observers to rate the various speakers as either charismatic or non-charismatic. Certain speakers such as Rosabeth Moss Kanter and management professor Gary Hamel were rated as animated, dynamic, charismatic. Others, such as Stephen Covey and Daniel Goleman, were rated as more low-key and decidedly non-charismatic.

The scholars then spent hours and hours analysing videos of each speaker, painstakingly coding their speeches one sentence at a time for the presence of up to six distinct nonverbal cues:

1. The speaker was gazing at the audience.

2. The sentence was delivered more loudly than surrounding speech material.
3. The sentence was delivered with a conspicuous speeding up, slowing down or some other shift in rhythm.
4. The sentence was spoken with either greater pitch or stress.
5. The sentence was spoken at the same time as the use of facial, hand and/or body gestures.
6. The sentence was delivered as the speaker walked around the stage or auditorium.

A sentence was awarded an impact score of zero if none of the six cues was present. One cue was taken as evidence of low impact, two cues as intermediate impact and three or more as high impact.

Thankfully for the researchers, given their many, many hours of video analysis, they discovered a clear pattern. Charismatic speakers tended to utilize significantly more of the speaking features than non-charismatic speakers did.

Interestingly, though, more cues was not always better. For example, management authority Tom Peters was rated by many observers as charismatic. Yet he was slated a lot of the time too. A whopping 47 per cent of observers complained that his speaking style was "too fast paced", "overly energetic" or even "aggressive".

Too many nonverbal cues may inadvertently convey the wrong impression.

Instead, those who were classified as charismatic – but not over the top – used a mere 2.23 cues per sentence. So that may mean uniting any two of the six features most of the time and perhaps using a few more occasionally. But it definitely did not mean using all six of the features all of the time. No, too many nonverbal cues may inadvertently convey the wrong impression.

Last year, I watched a speaker I'll call Oliver Entwhistle. A short man in a suit that swamped his small frame, he had a shock of white hair that, seemingly in defiance of gravity, rose several inches above his head. He introduced himself as an ex-business owner, author and now business consultant.

Speaking in a disconcertingly deep voice, he regaled us with stories of entrepreneurs and business owners that he had encountered. For example, a husband-and-wife partnership that had reported feeling overworked and in the doldrums in both their professional and personal lives until they had taken guidance from the consultancy for which he now worked. Clearly, he was making a sales pitch.

But there was something slightly off-key about his presentation. After about 20 minutes, I was starting to feel a bit jittery and happened to make eye contact with the audience member sitting next to me. A woman running a small physiotherapy business, she articulated what I had been thinking. Conspiratorially, she whispered, "I don't trust him. He's too sales-y."

And he was. He struck me as too slick, calculating, oleaginous.

Perhaps the trouble was that he was so rehearsed and polished that it no longer felt genuine. He stared out at the audience with an almost manic degree of focus. Nearly every other word was overpronounced. Lingering pauses were introduced at just the right moments to create a sense of drama. His every movement – the chopping gestures he made with his hands, the disappointed shakes he gave with his head, his occasional sighs of mock exasperation – was so emphatic. He had so much zeal you may have thought he was trying to save our souls from fiery damnation, not sell us the services of a business-to-business consultancy.

It's rare that I encounter individuals who exhibit too many nonverbal cues. The far commoner issue is that most people don't use enough of them. But Entwhistle was a clear exemplar of someone who came across as inauthentic partly because he had simply piled on too many nonverbal cues. Too much was going on when he spoke.

But back to the study by Clark and Greatbatch. I think it's worth taking a few moments to spell out the ramifications of their findings. What exactly does it mean for us?

For starters, it corroborates the importance of nonverbal behaviour in determining impact and charisma. Nonverbal cues make a difference.

We should aspire to use nonverbal cues relatively sparingly.

However, it's worth bearing in mind that we should aspire to use nonverbal cues relatively sparingly rather than throwing everything at an audience all of the time. It's like the story of Goldilocks and the Three Bears. Speakers who employ too few nonverbal cues tend to get rated rather poorly by audiences. Speakers who flaunt too many nonverbal features get criticized for being excessively animated. So it's people who use nonverbal cues that are "just right" (or, to be more precise, 2.23 cues per sentence) who make the optimal impact.

Developing your personal style

Take a look back at the six nonverbal cues investigated by Timothy Clark and David Greatbatch:

- Eye contact with your audience.
- Emphasizing a particular word or phrase by saying it more loudly.

- Speaking a word or phrase distinctly faster or slower than usual.
- Using pitch to emphasize a word, e.g. by going up or down in tone.
- Using facial expressions or gestures to accompany what you're saying.
- Walking around a room.

Clearly, none of these should be a surprise. Intellectually, we *all* understand that these cues are important. Why, then, doesn't *everybody* use them? Answer: because there's often a big gap between understanding and application. So the next time you speak – whether that's in a one-to-one discussion or presenting to an audience of many – think about the cues you want to introduce into your performance.

Matching your message

The six nonverbal cues we've encountered may be somewhat helpful. But when and how should you use them exactly?

To explain some unifying principles, I'd like to invite you to envision for a moment that you're a sales assistant in a heavy electrical goods shop. So you specialize in selling flat-screen TVs, computers, washing machines, refrigerators and dishwashers.

A customer – a man in his mid-30s – approaches you and says he's looking for a new washing machine. He's been looking at a machine that seems to have all of the functions he and his family need. A cardboard plaque on the machine says it has a large internal capacity so he can put the entire family's clothes in it. It's also highly energy efficient and so uses less electricity than many other models. Best of all, it's roughly half the price of other models he's been looking at.

The only catch: it's made by a Chinese manufacturer he's never heard of before.

You work on commission so you're hoping to make the sale. If you had to pick one overall nonverbal style, which of the following would you pick?

Here's a brief description of each:

- **Eager style** – using lots of open gestures with your palms up and hands projecting away from your body. This nonverbal style also means leaning towards a customer, using relatively fast, fluid body movements and speaking fairly quickly. The aim is to convey energy, dynamism, eagerness.
- **Vigilant style** – using fewer gestures, keeping your palms facing down and generally keeping your hands closer to your body. This style also means leaning slightly away from a customer, using relatively slow, precise body movements and speaking more slowly. Your aim is to convey respect, caution and attention to detail.[16]

So which would you go for? Would you be eager and upbeat? Or vigilant and more deferential?

Our decision-making is influenced in different directions by approach versus avoidance forces.

Actually, it's a bit of a trick question as neither is inherently better. Before I explain why, let me introduce a further set of concepts known as "approach factors and avoidance factors". Broadly speaking, psychologists say that our decision-making is influenced in different directions by approach versus avoidance forces.

Approach factors are the advantages, or pros, that make a course of action more desirable. For example, learning that a washing machine has a very large drum and could take up to 10kg of clothing at a time makes it more desirable. The fact that the washing machine has a dizzying spin speed of 2400 revolutions per minute also means that it can dry clothes more efficiently than many other machines too. And being half the price of course makes it extremely attractive too. So approach factors include all of the appealing features and benefits that make people ache to say "Yes."

Avoidance factors, on the other hand, are the issues, or cons, that may cause customers to shy away from – or avoid – a course of action. So the fact that the customer hasn't heard of a brand before may be a concern. He may also be worried that, should the machine go wrong, the parts will be troublesome to find or expensive to buy. In sum, avoidance factors consist of all of the doubts and concerns that may make people want to hold back or walk away entirely.

Coming back to the question of which nonverbal style you should choose to seal the deal, the answer is that it *depends*. No one nonverbal style suits all situations. Being energetic and upbeat could as easily turn away some customers as win over others.

Success at persuading nonverbally is about matching your style to someone's desires and concerns. So take a guess. If, during the conversation, you discover that the customer is more focused on the features and benefits – the approach factors – which style would be more effective? Or if he says he's worried about his lack of familiarity with the brand and concerned about what could go wrong, which style would be better?

Studies by Dutch research collaborators Bob Fennis at the University of Groningen and Marielle Stel from Tilburg University suggest that adopting the eager style – i.e. behaving in an

No one nonverbal style suits all situations.

upbeat, energetic and dynamic fashion – can bolster our persuasiveness when we're extolling the virtues of a product or idea. When we're talking up cool features and benefits, we may be better off showing that we're keen and enthusiastic about what we're offering. So that means allowing more exuberance to creep into our voices, gesturing more and perhaps leaning in towards an audience.

On the other hand, if you find that the customer is much more worried about his lack of familiarity with the brand and concerned about what could go wrong, you would be wise to play things more calmly. When we're trying to assuage the doubts of an audience, tackle their objections and minimize avoidance factors, we may be more successful by adopting the more downbeat and deadly serious vigilant nonverbal manner. Perhaps that means speaking slightly more slowly, using fewer and smaller gestures and being more respectful of people's personal space.[17]

Here's a speedy summary of the two.

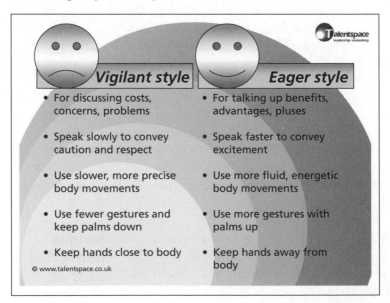

Vigilant style

- For discussing costs, concerns, problems
- Speak slowly to convey caution and respect
- Use slower, more precise body movements
- Use fewer gestures and keep palms down
- Keep hands close to body

© www.talentspace.co.uk

Eager style

- For talking up benefits, advantages, pluses
- Speak faster to convey excitement
- Use more fluid, energetic body movements
- Use more gestures with palms up
- Keep hands away from body

Match your nonverbal style to fit your message and you may boost its persuasiveness. Get it wrong by choosing a nonverbal style that clashes with your message and you may produce a phenomenon that psychologists call "source confusion". No prizes for guessing that this is not a good thing.[18]

For instance, suppose you are selling corporate insurance against the risks of fire or the collapse of the financial markets or anything else going awry. You could inadvertently distract a customer or client by being upbeat. Your audience may not even consciously be aware of why they're not warming to you. They may somehow find you a little unnerving, unbalanced and just wrong for them. But speaking more slowly and generally being somewhat dour may lend you more presence and gravitas.

I'll finish by giving you a final example. Consider an experimental trial in which the distinguished pairing of Northwestern University psychologist Angela Lee and Stanford University professor Jennifer Aaker presented audiences with advertisements for a made-up grape juice drink. In pitching the drink to different audiences, the investigators emphasized either its energy-boosting benefits or its disease-preventing properties.[19]

Match your nonverbal style to fit your message and you may boost Its persuasiveness.

Imagine for a moment that it's *you* who has to pitch the drink to an audience. How would you behave in order to point up each different angle?

I'm sure you get the point by now. If you had to stress its energy-boosting effects, you'd smile, allow your voice to soar and dip; you'd be lively and animated too. On the other hand, if you wanted to highlight the fact that drinking it could stave off illness, you would be better off using less inflection in your voice, adopting more measured facial expressions and being fairly economical with your gestures and movement.

To finish off, here's a side-by-side comparison of the two nonverbal styles:[20]

Use an eager, animated nonverbal style when...	Use a vigilant, precise nonverbal style when...
You're talking about the attractive features, advantages and benefits of an idea, product or service.	You're trying to reassure someone about the costs, limitations or potential problems associated with an idea, product or service.
You may be looking to promote a desirable behaviour such as eating more fruit and vegetables.	You may be looking to prevent a bad habit or behaviour such as eating sugary foods.
You're helping someone to achieve a positive outcome. For example, you may be telling a friend to give up smoking because it would allow her to run up multiple flights of stairs and not get out of breath!	You're helping someone to avoid a negative outcome. For example, you may be telling a friend to give up smoking because it may otherwise lead to lung cancer, emphysema and an earlier death.
You're encouraging an audience to take risks and aim high.	You're imploring an audience to play it safe and avoid mistakes.
You're encouraging someone to do something because of the opportunities, fun or perks that may be associated with it. You're talking about carrots rather than sticks – you are emphasizing the rewards associated with doing it.	You're warning someone about the hazards, risks or dangers of not doing something. This is more about sticks than carrots – there may be either subtle or brazen threats of punishments or censure for not doing it.

Use an eager, animated nonverbal style when...	Use a vigilant, precise nonverbal style when...
For instance, you may want your workmates to use a new method at work because it will lead to customers being more satisfied.	For instance, you may insist your workmates use a new method at work because otherwise problems will arise and customers will make more complaints.
You are tapping into your audience's hopes and dreams – things they *want* to do.	You are making your audience think about duties and obligations – things they *should* do.

Building your nonverbal repertoire

As we come to the close of the chapter, I hope I have demonstrated that nonverbal tactics matter. But what you may need to work on depends on your natural strengths.

Remember the nonverbal expressiveness questionnaire we encountered towards the start of this chapter? It's probably a bit of a cliché to hear a psychologist like me say that there are no right or wrong answers, but in this case it's true.

If you score high on nonverbal expressiveness, you may naturally find it easier to adopt the eager style with its energetic, animated use of voice, face and movement. But when you need to be calmer and more respectful – discussing a grievous error or profit warning, for example – you may find it harder to keep your mannerisms in check. If you don't, you may risk coming across as overblown or phony.

In contrast, if you score low on nonverbal expressiveness, you may feel more comfortable deploying the vigilant style that is characterized by a steadier and more composed voice, face and all-round movement. But when it becomes time to deliver a fun, upbeat message, such as the launch of a new product, you could perhaps do with making more of an effort to turn up the dial on your use of nonverbal tactics.

What you may need to work on depends on your natural strengths. No one style trumps all. But the point is this: becoming more aware of your nonverbal communication is an excellent starting point in becoming a more compelling speaker, negotiator, trade show vendor, whatever. Taking a few minutes to understand an audience – whether it's one needy friend, a sceptical shareholder or a mob of unruly customers – and thinking about the right nonverbal style to adopt could help you to stand out for all the right reasons.

The sometimes baffling array of nonverbal behaviours that make up charisma can be learnt, worked upon, honed. When will you start?

Pulling everything together

Here are three final pointers on using nonverbal cues to make a breath-taking impact:

- **Ask for candid comments on your nonverbal strengths and weaknesses.** Many people overestimate their effectiveness, while some underestimate it. Few people have a clear understanding of exactly what they're good and not so good at. So ask teammates, friends and family members for comments on how you genuinely come across. Encourage them to be super-candid in their appraisals of you – scathingly so if necessary. Are you someone who has an overly passive face? Are you too quiet or monotone? Should you inject more energy into your presentations or calm down a bit? Only by asking those around you for their honest thoughts can you establish exactly what you need to work on.

- **Rehearse, rehearse, rehearse what you want to say.** Before you can work on your gestures, tone of voice or anything else, you should be very familiar with the content of your pitch or the structure of the conversation you'd like to have. The human brain has a fairly limited processing capacity. So if you're struggling to remember *what* you're saying, it's unlikely you'll be able to focus on *how* you come across. Once you know your material, you can then divert much more of your attention to your nonverbal impact.

- **Record a rehearsal.** Use a video camera – for example the one on your smartphone – to record yourself delivering the first 10 minutes of what you wish to say. Play it back and look out for just three things you could do differently. Write down three action statements for what you wish to do differently. Why three? In practice, most people I work with find that it's a manageable number. Many more and you can give yourself too much to do.

Interpreting individual facial cues

Earlier in the chapter, I presented you with a table of nonverbal cues and invited you to have a go at interpreting their meanings. Here's the table of the different cues with their alleged meanings in full.

Nonverbal cue	Meaning
Head nod	Acceptance of what's being said or done
Head nod + smile	Liking

(Continued)

89

Nonverbal cue	Meaning
Tilt head to side + sad eyebrows	Lack of understanding
Eye roll	Disbelief
Tilt head to side + gaze down	Boredom
Shake head + frown + tense lips	Disagreement/rejection
Head shake	Rejection of what's being said or done
Head shake + frown	Disagreement, rejection
Tilt head to side + frown	Disagreement, disbelief
Eyes wide open	Disbelief

Onwards and upwards

- Understand that there's a fairly overwhelming deluge of evidence showing that nonverbal cues – everything from facial expressions and the qualities of your voice to your every bodily movement – can make a quantifiable difference to your charisma, your memorability and your impact.
- In terms of vocal traits, remember that speaking in a lower pitch may help you to be perceived as more leader-like, competent and trustworthy. Consider also the somewhat unexpected finding that speaking more quickly tends to be associated with better ratings too.
- Weave more gestures into your behaviour if you would like to improve your persuasiveness. However, remember that not all gestures are created equal: gestures that involve touching yourself may signify self-doubt or deception.
- Remember to match your overall nonverbal style to the nature of the message you wish to deliver. Being dynamic and energetic is not always appropriate. Consider when you may need

to tone things down too. There is no absolute right or wrong nonverbal style – only what works best for any given situation.

- Ask people for feedback on the appropriateness of your style. Yes, most folks could do with becoming more nonverbally expressive. But you may just be in that minority which needs to cool things down a bit. Don't assume you know what you need to work on. Encourage those around you to tell you what you may not realize about yourself.

3

Winning with Words

The object of oratory alone is not truth, but persuasion.
Thomas Babington Macaulay

Here's a thought experiment for you. If you could change the behaviour of an individual or a group of people, who would they be and what would you have them doing differently?

I posed this question to five friends over lunch on a sunshiny Sunday afternoon and got the following responses:

1. "I'd help my father to find the personal motivation to exercise and lose weight."
2. "Simple one this! It would be my bosses and directors and I would ask them to open their eyes and listen to their employees. We're the closest to the customers and know what they want."
3. "I would sit world leaders down to understand the severity of the threat of climate change. They're not leaving the room until they agree serious plans on how to decarbonize the world economy."
4. "I wish doctors listened better. Since their diagnosis is dependent on the information elicited from a patient, it would be useful if they had more training in how to establish trust and to question effectively."

5. "My brother is screwing up our family at the moment feuding with my sister and brutalizing our mother. I would want to get him to see the family as a set of core nurturing relationships, trust that we are all good people, keep his cool, listen and seek to create authentic resolution to the conflict."

So what would your aims be?

Perhaps your hope is to alter the behaviour of a single loved one, a friend or family member (as shown in examples 1 and 5). It could be that you are feeling frustrated by colleagues and wish they would behave differently (example 2). Maybe you wish to woo benefactors for a charity, supporters for a cause (example 3) or investors for your embryonic business. Or perhaps you want to alter the behaviour of a specific group (example 4), a community or even society as a whole.

I know from emails and tweets I've received that a lot of the readers of my books are sales professionals, entrepreneurs or the owners of small businesses hungry to land customers and clients. You could be a politician eager to win over the public, a manager striving to motivate a team or a lawyer hoping to sway a jury in court.

Your audience could be a single individual or a handful of people sitting in an office or around a kitchen table. It could be a crowd in an auditorium or perhaps even millions through live television or a video uploaded to YouTube, for example.

Want to know how you can almost guarantee to fall short in your aims? To have your wishes totally ignored?

Stick to a compelling argument. Simply describe the problem and its logical solution. Perhaps identify likely objections, worries or niggles and include good reasons why such opposition is unjustified.

Or, if you're trying to get people to pursue an opportunity, describe your proposal and the rational reasoning behind it.

Yes, if you want your words to fall on deaf ears, rely on a barrage of facts and statistics. Try to boost your credibility only by bombarding someone with data, numbers, charts and the indisputable logic of your case.

If you want your words to fall on deaf ears, rely on a barrage of facts and statistics.

Consider smokers, for example. The vast majority of smokers in the Western world know by now that smoking can cause cancer and other diseases. But they choose to smoke regardless. So if you want to fail to change the behaviour of friends or loved ones who smoke, by all means toss more statistics at them. If you're a government agency trying to save millions of lives, go ahead and keep quoting the same old facts over and over again.

Or think about the case for changing all of the lightbulbs in people's homes for energy-saving bulbs. The financial justification is clear: energy-efficient bulbs cut electricity bills. Over time, they not only recoup the initial investment in new bulbs but save homeowners even more money month after month after month. Why, then, haven't people made the switch? Because they can grasp a line of reasoning but still not feel it psychologically worthwhile to budge in how they behave.

You can probably come up with your own examples. Time after time, you will have seen for yourself that a fusillade of facts and figures alone hardly ever wins people over. A carefully constructed, logical argument may have heads nodding in agreement but still be insufficient to get them to change. To shift how people behave, you need to give them more.

You have to smuggle past people's defences and get them to care enough to pay attention. The only question is: how?

95

Starting with your audience

Imagine for a moment that you're pitching a radical new idea to an audience of potential buyers. It's a concept that is genuinely new – it's never been seen or done before anywhere in the country. Of course, you can understand that your audience may be a bit twitchy, rather wary.

That's only half of the challenge, though. There's a further complication, making it even more improbable that the already cautious buyers will say yes. You're not only asking them to give you a chance but to give you millions of pounds *up front*. Just on trust. Oh, and the buyers won't see the product until many months later.

Now *that* is a tough sell.

But that's precisely what Jim Sayer has to do, because he works in the cutthroat world of television. To be successful, a TV production company has to tempt a buyer – that could be an individual or a roomful of television executives – to stump up a walloping sum of money merely on the *promise* of an interesting TV programme or series at the end of it.

I first worked with television producer Sayer over a decade ago when he was an executive-for-hire. In the intervening years, he has risen up the ranks to become first managing director and now chief executive of BAFTA and Emmy-award-winning television and media production company Maverick TV.

Maverick TV has multiple offices in both the UK and US and is perhaps best known in the UK for *Embarrassing Bodies*, the notorious Channel 4 show that regularly beams unflinching, often close-up shots of vaginas, penises and anuses over the airwaves during primetime. For all its scandalous content, the programme has undoubtedly helped to demystify many ailments, encouraged millions of viewers to be more aware of their health and probably even saved a few lives.

Branded content is another area of expertise for the company. Businesses such as Microsoft and Marks & Spencer as well as public sector organizations and even charities pay for highly polished short films designed to champion their products or causes.

Over the course of his career, Sayer has pitched possibly hundreds of ideas for documentaries, game shows, children's programmes, advertising campaigns and fund-raising films.

Dressed in jeans and a pressed shirt, Sayer had just the right amount of stubble on his somewhat boyish face to mark him out as a modish television executive. An impish grin frequently crossed his face as we spoke.

So what is the key to success in winning over cagey buyers in the world of television?

"It's about trying to understand a buyer," he said.

Buyers at TV networks in the US, for example, tend to demand slick presentations accompanied by polished PowerPoint slides. There's little pretence that it's anything but a sales meeting.

To stand out, think more about the individual needs of each particular audience.

"There can be two minutes of chit-chat and pleasantries at the beginning followed by the words 'What have you got?' and then normally there's an expectation that they will be seeing a formal pitch," he explained.

In contrast, broadcasters in the UK typically crave more of a conversation. It isn't unusual for Sayer to end up asking as many questions as he is expected to answer.

"To pitch in the UK is about really thinking carefully about who you're going to see and what it is they're likely to want. So it's a process of getting to know a buyer and knowing their particular predilections in terms of television," he added.

"One of the things broadcasters worry about, quite rightly, is whether you understand that channel. You may do lots of stuff for Channel 4, but do you understand the BBC or ITV or Sky audience? That's really important and something you have to demonstrate in the pitch."

Buyers at non-television organizations need different treatment again. Organizations such as charities and government agencies are often far less sophisticated in their understanding of how to produce engaging films or online content.

Sayer recounted a time he pitched to produce a fund-raising film for the Private Equity Foundation, a charity which has since been renamed as Impetus – The Private Equity Foundation. In trying to give the charity's chief executive an idea of the kind of film he was offering to produce, he referred to various television programmes with a similar tone.

When the chief executive commented on his pitch, her response wasn't quite what he was looking for. "At the end, the chief executive said to me, 'I should probably let you know that I don't own a television.' I've never been that wrong-footed before or since in a meeting because I realized that all of the things I had assumed she would have seen she simply hadn't seen," laughed Sayer.

Considering the expectations that each of his audiences may have of him, Sayer even thinks about how to dress for greatest impact. Sometimes, he will wear a suit. When pitching to perhaps more staid organizations, he doesn't want them wondering why the chief executive of Maverick TV is dressed like he may be off to the pub for a weekend drink with mates.

"Sometimes, there's genuine value in turning up in jeans and a t-shirt, because what they're buying from you is something they know they don't have for themselves. And so one of the things you have to judge is which of the two things it is. Should I wear a suit or should I wear what I normally wear for work?" he explained.

What is clear from Sayer's recollections are that different audiences need very different pitches. US TV executives differ from their British counterparts, while non-broadcasting organizations may require considerably more handholding. So does an audience need a formal presentation or more of a conversation? What kind of language and shared points of reference would be appropriate? Even what kind of clothing might make an admirable impression or go down in flames?

To stand out, we would all do well to think more about the individual needs of each particular audience. Trotting out the same spiel again and again simply can't take into account the different hopes, fears, experiences and circumstances of each audience.

It may seem like a no-brainer to say that we need to think about the audience first. But how many speakers actually do that? In my experience, not enough. Too many speakers think about what they want to say rather than what may help an audience take on board a message.

Audiences can differ on all sorts of variables. And when I say audience, that could be a lecture theatre of students, a conference venue crammed with co-workers or a single investor or customer sitting at a boardroom table.

Let's consider one of the commonest demographic variables: men versus women. Are men in an audience persuaded any differently from women?

Too many speakers think about what they want to say rather than what may help an audience take on board a message.

99

Testing this question – one that is potentially fraught with gender politics – psychological scientists Nicole Mayer from the University of Illinois at Chicago and Zakary Tormala from Stanford University conducted an uncomplicated yet revealing experiment. Their goal: to convince men versus women that a fictitious movie called *The Inventor* was worth watching.

They put together a number of reviews as follows:

Greg Blasius, *Charlotte Observer*: "I feel that this will be a winner, a must-have for any film collector!"

Nanci Fyffe, *Variety Film Magazine*: "Masterfully done! You can really feel what this guy was going through."

Shari Nugara, *Film Dossier International*: "An alluring delight that is sure to capture the interest of all audiences."

Frederick Lerner, movieview.com: "My feeling is that this trumps nearly every movie of its kind in the last 10 years."

Based on those four reviews, how much do you think you would like the movie? The participants in the study were asked to rate the movie on a scale ranging from 1 ("not at all") to 9 ("very much").

Now, consider what score you would have given the movie had you read these similar but not quite identical reviews:

Greg Blasius, *Charlotte Observer*: "I think that this will be a winner, a must-have for any film collector!"

Nanci Fyffe, *Variety Film Magazine*: "Masterfully done! It makes you really think what this guy was going through."

Shari Nugara, *Film Dossier International*: "An alluring delight that is sure to capture the interest of all audiences."

Frederick Lerner, movieview.com: "My thought is that this trumps nearly every movie of its kind in the last 10 years."

Spot the difference? In the first set of quotes, there's an emphasis on *feeling* with the word "feel" cropping up twice and "feeling" appearing once. In the second set, the emphasis is on *thinking*: "think" pops up a couple of times and "thinking" is used once.

You probably won't be influenced any differently because I've shown you both sets of reviews. But when Mayer and Tomala shared the *thinking* versus *feeling* quotes to groups of either men or women, they found an interesting difference.

Men said that they liked the movie more when the reviews were framed in terms of thinking. Women preferred the movie when the reviews were framed in terms of feeling.[1]

Now the researchers were quite clear: this doesn't mean that women are less *able* to think than men. However, other studies do confirm that women on average report experiencing more intense emotions than men do.[2] There's even evidence that women tend to be more attuned to the emotions of others than men are.[3] Whether it's down to differences in nature or nurture – innate differences between the sexes or how they are raised – we don't know.

Men and women do seem to be influenced differently.

But the lesson is clear. If you're speaking to a man or a group of men, emphasize your analytical, or so-called cognitive, stance by including words such as "think", "thinking" and "thought". On the other hand, if you're dealing with a woman or group of women, you may be better off highlighting the emotional, or so-called affective, aspects of your argument by using words such as "feel", "feeling" and "felt".

Of course, this study doesn't mean that all men are more influenced by thinking cues and all women by feeling cues. It only says that men are *generally* more influenced by calls to action that emphasize thinking while women are *generally* more influenced by messages that focus on feeling. If you get to know people well, you are almost guaranteed to discover that certain men you're acquainted with rely more heavily on their feelings and that particular women respond better to analysis and logic. But in the absence of more valuable information about a potential audience, understanding that men and women do seem to be influenced differently could be a useful place to start when you are vying for people's attention.

Of course there are many ways in which people differ from each other. In our continuing quest to make an impact, let's consider another demographic factor: the cultural background of an audience. Social scientists have long suspected that Western cultures (such as in the United Kingdom, Australia, Western Europe and the United States) tend to be more individualistic in nature than Eastern cultures (such as in China, India, Taiwan and Vietnam), which tend to be more collectivistic. For example, a 1994 analysis of print advertisements in the US versus Korea by researchers Sang-Pil Han at Hanyang University in Korea and Sharon Shavitt at the University of Illinois, Urbana-Champaign found that US magazine advertisements tended to appeal to individualistic values such as personal success, independence and individual benefits. In contrast, advertisements from similar magazines in Korea most commonly emphasized shared benefits, group harmony and family integrity.[4]

Now you might expect that tailoring a warning to the cultural background of your audience would buttress the effectiveness – the sheer persuasiveness – of your message. But things aren't quite that simple.

Let's look at another study, this time by social science mavens Ayse Uskul from the University of Essex and Daphna Oyserman from the University of Michigan. These researchers began by creating two very similar health articles for either European American or Asian American audiences.

Both articles from a fictitious *Health Today Newsletter* alleged a link between caffeine consumption and fibrocystic disease. One version emphasized the impact that the disease had on individuals. The second version highlighted the impact that the disease had on relationships, i.e. on collective units.

Now you might expect that individualistic European Americans would have been more swayed by the advice that drew attention to the harm it could do to individuals. And you might expect that Asian Americans – folks who hailed from China, Korea, Taiwan and Vietnam, for example – would have been more influenced by the note that underscored how the disease could turn you into a burden for your family.

But no. There was no such effect.

It was only when audiences were *reminded* of – or in the psychological parlance *primed* as to – their individualistic or collectivistic cultural background that the messages became more potent. In other words, the European Americans had to be presented with pronouns that emphasized individuality such as "I", "mine" and "me"; the Asian Americans had to be presented with pronouns such as "we", "our" and "us".[5]

So let's say you're trying to win over two individuals who come from different parts of the world. Suppose Artie hails from the UK or Australia. You would need to prime him by using more language like "I" and "me" before pointing out how a course of action might benefit him as an individual. But if you're attempting to win an endorsement from Xiaopang, a guy from China or Taiwan, you would need to prime him with "we" and "us" before emphasizing how the same course of action might benefit his family, his community and his organization.

Having your audience in mind

Inexperienced speakers often focus on what they want to communicate rather than what an audience may be ready to hear. That's hardly surprising. We're all so busy that we tend to think of our own concerns and what we are hoping to achieve in putting together a speech, pitch or press release. But the truth is that the very best presenters, salespeople and conversationalists consider the audience's concerns, interests and emotions first:

- **Think about the demographics of your audience.** Clearly, not all men are persuaded in the same way, just as all women are not the same. Likewise, not everybody from a particular country is the same. But generally speaking it's worth thinking about how factors such as gender, culture, religious background, age, educational level, class and other factors may affect your audience.
- **Consider what your audience is thinking.** What concerns or issues are your audience most interested in? Are there problems they're wrestling with or opportunities they would love to pursue?
- **Consider how your audience is feeling.** Are they ecstatic to be there or have they been forced to attend and therefore sceptical or even enraged? Are they disappointed, frustrated, restless or something else?
- **Ask yourself what your audience may know about *you*.** How much do they know about you, your background and expertise? To what extent do you need to introduce yourself and explain your credibility or interest in this topic?

The more you can see the world from the perspectives of others, the more you can tailor your messages for maximum persuasion. Understanding the starting point of your audience may well help you identify the best approach to get them where you would like them to be.

Perhaps you're still thinking that you haven't learnt anything new, that surely everybody knows that they should always start from the viewpoint of our audiences. But I don't think that's the case.

I've sat through countless bad presentations – *and I'm sure you have too.* Presentations in which speakers were just sprinkling numbers and reasons at an audience with scant consideration for their particular needs. But then it's easier to do that, isn't it? It takes a lot of work to consider each individual audience, to glean their needs and tailor a presentation accordingly.

Treating all audiences as the same is ultimately a shortcut to nowhere.

But I would contend that that is an illusory way to save time. Treating all audiences as the same is ultimately a shortcut to nowhere.

Tapping into the persuasive power of emotion

Jim Sayer at Maverick TV asserts that his television and media business is perhaps more about winning hearts than minds. When we discussed his tack when it comes to creating fundraising films for charities, for example, he said: "What we're about is an emotional engagement. If you get the emotional engagement, the money will come pouring in. That's what [charitable] giving is about. No one gives because they like the sound of the charity. They give because they've had an emotional experience."

Perhaps that's true of fundraising when you're trying to entice people to put their hands in their pockets for disadvantaged children, mistreated animals, abused women and the like. But what about in other disciplines?

Surely business investors or customers are more sensible and hard-headed? Surely the voting public decides whether or not to vote by rationally weighing the possible inconvenience of going to the ballot box against the potential benefits of electing someone they like?

Let's take that second example and look at what the science tells us. First, though, some background about voting.

In many democracies, the share of people voting has been falling. For example, the percentage of the British population that voted in general elections has fallen rather precipitously over the decades. In 1950, 83.9 per cent of adults voted. In 2010, that figure had slumped to 65.1 per cent.[6]

In the US, the decline has been less steep. In 1952, 63.3 per cent of American adults cast a vote in the Presidential election. In 2008, only 57.5 per cent cared enough to vote.

A minority of countries like Australia, Belgium and Chile have solved the problem by instituting compulsory voting: fail to vote and you may get fined or even sent to jail. But in most democracies around the world, governments and lobbyists alike have wondered how they can encourage more of society to vote.

How would *you* encourage more voters?

Political scientist Costas Panagopoulos at Fordham University in New York may just have found an answer. Taking advantage of municipal elections going on across the country in 2007, he chose to send different postcards to the inhabitants of two cities in the state of Iowa.[7]

Several weeks before the election, he sent out one version of a postcard to several hundred households in the city of Monticello, Iowa. This version was intended to inspire in people a sense of pride should they vote:

WHO VOTES IS PUBLIC INFORMATION!

Dear registered voter:

On November 6, 2007, an election to select local leaders will be held in Monticello, IA.

As a registered voter, you are eligible to vote in this election. We urge you to exercise your civic duty and vote on November 6.

We also remind you that who votes is a matter of public record.

To honor those who take time to vote in the upcoming election, we will obtain a complete list of registered voters who cast ballots on Election Day from local election officials in Monticello and publish their names in the local newspaper.

The names of voters who did not vote will not be published because only voters deserve special recognition.

DO YOUR CIVIC DUTY! VOTE ON ELECTION DAY!

Panagopoulos then chose to send a slightly different postcard out to several hundred households in the city of Ely, also in Iowa. This version was intended to instil in people a sense of shame should they *not* vote:

WHO VOTES IS PUBLIC INFORMATION!

Dear registered voter:

On November 6, 2007, an election to select local leaders will be held in Ely, IA.

(Continued)

As a registered voter, you are eligible to vote in this election. We urge you to exercise your civic duty and vote on November 6.

We also remind you that who votes is a matter of public record.

To promote participation in the election, we will obtain a complete list of registered voters who cast ballots on Election Day from local election officials. Shortly after the November 2007 election, we will publish in a local newspaper a complete list of all Ely registered voters who did not vote.

The names of those who took the time to vote will <u>not</u> appear on this list.

DO YOUR CIVIC DUTY! VOTE ON ELECTION DAY!

Compare the two postcards and you can spot the difference. The first offers to highlight those who *did* vote. The second threatens to draw attention to those who *didn't* vote.

Immediately after the elections, Panagopoulos obtained validated voter turnout data to see whether his postcards had had any effect. So what do you think transpired? Would you be more inspired to vote by a sense of pride in being recognized for having voted? Or would you be more motivated to vote in order to avoid the sense of shame in being called out for *not* having voted?

When Panagopoulos compared the voting patterns of the households in his study, he found that people who had received the pride postcard were 4.7 per cent more likely to vote than other households in the same city that had not received the postcard. So yes, pride did coax more people into voting.

More strikingly, though, people who had received the shame postcard were 6.9 per cent more likely to vote than households in the same city that had not received any postcard. So shame had been an even sturdier and more bluntly potent emotion.

Now the percentages in Panagopoulos's investigation may seem tiny, trivial, almost not worth bothering about. But remember that this was just a single postcard that was sent out. It probably took homeowners mere seconds to read

Imagine how powerfully you might be able to use emotion.

before discarding it in the bin. But even the merest *insinuation* that they might receive special recognition or infamy was enough to produce a measurable effect. So imagine how powerfully you might be able to use emotion in your presentations, negotiations and conversations when people are spending much longer with you.

Economists have for decades argued that human beings act as rational individuals, making decisions predicated on a hard-headed weighing-up of costs and benefits. But psychologists know differently. Emotions such as love, guilt, anger, joy, worry and grief – as well as pride or shame – can drive our behaviour in all sorts of ways.

Love, guilt, anger, joy, worry and grief – as well as pride or shame – can drive our behaviour.

It seems that it doesn't really matter whether an emotion is broadly positive or negative. Remember in Panagopoulos's study that the postcards either tapped into the positive emotion of pride or the negative emotion of shame. Yes, shame was more effective in that instance, but actually *both* emotions persuaded more people to vote.

Engendering emotion

For good reason, impactful individuals aim to stir up emotions in their audiences. If you can make your audience feel

(Continued)

109

something – a gasp of surprise, a sneer of annoyance, a snort of disagreement – they may take your message to heart and do something differently.

My advice: think before you start writing your presentation or sales pitch about the *one* emotion you want to convey to your audience. Almost before you start putting pen to paper or creating your slide deck, consider the emotion you wish to bring about.

Is it excitement you aspire to stir up in a group of colleagues? Is it perhaps anger about some social injustice? Maybe you want a crowd to feel disgusted by an awful state of affairs – sufficiently sickened to do something about it. Another useful emotion is anxiety: to make people sufficiently worried about fixing some risk or predicament that they can't sleep at night. But don't be constrained by those emotions. Think broadly. Perhaps envy, hope, outrage, shame, trust, disgust, surprise, interest, pride, sadness or something else will work for you.

Once you've identified an emotion you think will work for a particular audience, you can keep reminding yourself of that single emotion as you prepare what you want to say. In practice, I've found that people who decide on an emotion *before* writing a presentation tend to convey it better than those who write a presentation first and *then* try to jam in an emotion.

A slew of studies tells us that emotional stimuli – speeches, TV commercials, stories, photographs and even postcards – tend to have a more vigorous impact than more neutral stimuli. Get people to laugh, cry or gnash their teeth and they talk, take action and buy. But the next emotion we will encounter stands apart from the rest. Handled well, it can galvanize a person, a group, even society into action. Used poorly, though, it can backfire completely.

Trading on terror

Imagine you're the chief executive of a monstrous business with tens of thousands of employees worldwide. The company has won dozens of awards for its products and has been written about in glowing terms in more newspaper and magazine articles than you can remember. But there's a change in the air. Over just the last couple of years, your competitors have been getting more tenacious and – almost without warning – your business is now on the back foot.

You have a plan, though. To reclaim your company's place at the head of the pack, you need your employees to work in a drastically different way. You're shrewd enough to know that simply telling them the situation and sharing a list of reasons for change will almost certainly fall on deaf ears. To create a real clarion call, you realize you need to evoke some real emotion – but which one?

Now you're weighing up two options. You could try to inspire them by presenting them an exciting picture of a scintillating future. Or you could scare them into believing that a failure to behave differently might result in tremendous job losses and doom.

What would you do?

This isn't a hypothetical scenario but a very real situation experienced by Nokia CEO Stephen Elop back in early 2011. If you can remember even further back to the year 2000, Nokia was *the* preeminent mobile phone company. Just about everyone had a Nokia mobile phone. Their phones were once cool. But over the decade of the noughties, Apple launched its wildly successful iPhone and Google developed its Android software platform.

By 2011, Nokia was an ailing business. It had lost its number-one position. Consumers no longer hankered after clunky Nokia phones.

Change was necessary if Nokia was to survive – let alone thrive. And Stephen Elop, a man with a reputation as a hard-charging leader who earned the nickname "The General", decided that he needed to scare his workforce into working differently.[8]

So he wrote his employees an email. We know all about the email because it was leaked to technology website Engadget.

After a relatively jaunty "Hello there" to open the letter, he continues with a modern-day parable:

> *There is a pertinent story about a man who was working on an oil platform in the North Sea. He woke up one night from a loud explosion, which suddenly set his entire oil platform on fire. In mere moments, he was surrounded by flames. Through the smoke and heat, he barely made his way out of the chaos to the platform's edge. When he looked down over the edge, all he could see were the dark, cold, foreboding Atlantic waters.*
>
> *As the fire approached him, the man had mere seconds to react. He could stand on the platform, and inevitably be consumed by the burning flames. Or, he could plunge 30 meters into the freezing waters. The man was standing upon a "burning platform," and he needed to make a choice.*
>
> *He decided to jump. It was unexpected. In ordinary circumstances, the man would never consider plunging into icy waters. But these were not ordinary times – his platform was on fire. The man survived the fall and the waters. After he was rescued, he noted that a "burning platform" caused a radical change in his behaviour.*
>
> *We, too, are standing on a "burning platform," and we must decide how we are going to change our behaviour.*

I won't reproduce the entire email, in the interests of space. There's a middle section in which Elop talks about the problems facing

Nokia. He uses scary phrases such as "we have multiple points of scorching heat that are fuelling a blazing fire around us". He prolongs the metaphor by saying there's "intense heat coming from our competitors" too.

The litany of woe goes on to say that consumer preference for Nokia phones has been plummeting worldwide. He cites, for example, that over the course of just a single year brand preference in the UK dropped from 28 per cent to only 20 per cent, meaning that a mere one in five Brits said they preferred Nokia to other brands. Anyway, you get the picture – you can go to the notes at the end of the book and find a link to the full missive if you like.[9] But he continues by asking:

Why did we fall behind when the world around us evolved?
This is what I have been trying to understand. I believe at least some of it has been due to our attitude inside Nokia. We poured gasoline on our own burning platform. I believe we have lacked accountability and leadership to align and direct the company through these disruptive times. We had a series of misses. We haven't been delivering innovation fast enough. We're not collaborating internally.
Nokia, our platform is burning.

It's not happy stuff, is it? The burning platform metaphor presents a terrifying choice. Either stay on the burning platform and surely suffer a painful and horrific death or jump into the waters far, far below. You may still die: you may drown, freeze to death in the icy waters or hit the water at the wrong angle and smash your body to pulp.

So it's either certain death or probable death. But Elop continues with the chilling scenario and finishes his email by saying:

I believe that together, we can face the challenges ahead of us. Together, we can choose to define our future.

The burning platform, upon which the man found himself, caused the man to shift his behaviour, and take a bold and brave step into an uncertain future. He was able to tell his story. Now, we have a great opportunity to do the same.

Stephen.

Imagine you're an employee working somewhere in the enormous behemoth that is Nokia. After reading that letter, how would you feel? Clearly, the tone of the email was negative. It was designed to scare employees, to make them sit up and take notice that it was time for a revamp. That if employees didn't jump off the burning platform, they would die. It was a pretty stark choice.

Sadly, history tells us that Elop's email failed to have its desired effect. Despite the fact he sent a very strong communiqué designed to frighten his workforce, his efforts didn't pay off.

I said in the previous section that emotion can drive behaviour. That almost any emotion can drive behaviour more effectively than cool-headed, rational argument alone. And fear is probably the mightiest emotion of them all. So why did Elop's email flop?

Fear is probably the mightiest emotion of them all. As luck would have it, we don't have to guess at an answer. Because psychologists and other social scientists have been investigating the effectiveness of so-called fear appeals for over 50 years. It's a crucial topic for study given that governments and public health practitioners want to promote healthy behaviours such as smoking cessation, use of sunscreen to prevent skin cancer, breast self-examinations, the eating of more fruits and vegetables, more physical exercise, dental flossing for oral hygiene and so on.

The leading theory of why certain fear appeals work – and why too many crash and burn – has been developed by Kim Witte, a professor of communication at Texas A&M University. Witte's Extended Parallel Process Model suggests that any fear appeal kicks off two sets of appraisals (mental calculations) of the message in an audience's mind.[10]

First, people weigh up the perceived threat at the heart of a call to action. Is this something that is both a *major* and *likely* threat? In our heads, mostly without us even consciously realizing it, we compute two initial appraisals:

> Appraisal 1a: Is this something that is significant – something that will have a major effect on my life?
>
> Appraisal 1b: Is this something that is likely to happen to me?

Suppose you're endeavouring to warn people about the importance of a healthy lifestyle in preventing heart disease. Our first patient: a 55-year-old dangerously obese man who has just been diagnosed with extremely high blood pressure. You tell him that if he doesn't do something to overhaul his lifestyle he may die. Given his age and weight, he is likely to perceive that the threat of a heart attack is both severe (Appraisal 1a) and that he is very likely to be affected (Appraisal 1b).

On the other hand, imagine trotting out the same warning to a svelte 25-year-old office worker who says she can eat pretty much anything she wants without putting on weight. Even though she may agree that the threat is potentially serious for many people (Appraisal 1a), she may feel that she is not personally at risk (Appraisal 1b). As a result, the message won't have any effect on her.

So the first step in creating an effective fear appeal is making sure that it, well, appeals to an audience. That it actually does engender fear in people. And so if you want to scare people into action, a threat has to seem both severe and relevant to people – they have to feel susceptible and personally affected. If they either feel that the consequences of a threat aren't that big a deal (Appraisal 1a) or that something doesn't really relate to them (Appraisal 1b), they're not going to be scared enough to take on board any fear appeal.

Then there's the second step, a second set of appraisals that people run through in their heads. And these are to do with the efficacy (effectiveness) of their response to the threat. Here, there are two further calculations:

Appraisal 2a: Is it likely that a response on my part will tackle the root cause of the fear?
Appraisal 2b: Is taking that action going to be easy?

Let's consider that painfully overweight 55-year-old guy with high blood pressure again for a moment. Suppose the doctor tells him that taking a daily pill will substantially reduce his risk of heart attack. If the patient reads elsewhere that the pills aren't actually that beneficial, he may fail to think that the answer to Appraisal 2a is "yes". He may have what's known as "low response efficacy" – he may think that the treatment simply isn't worth the bother. If that's the case, any fear appeal is likely to fail at this point.

Clearly, Appraisal 2a tells us that he needs to believe that the pills will be an effective solution. But even if he has this high response efficacy, he also needs to believe that he will actually be able to follow the advice that is being dispensed.

If you want to scare people into action, a threat has to seem both severe and relevant.

Appraisal 2b asks, "Is taking that action going to be easy?"

Clearly, if he only has to take a daily pill, that's very easy. The answer to the question is "yes". So he is likely to have high self-efficacy – or belief in his own ability to do what's required to mitigate the threat.

116

But imagine now that the guidance being given to him is different. That the doctor insists that he needs to make enormous adjustments in his lifestyle in order to ward off heart disease. He will have to cut out salt and sugar and saturated fat. He will have to renounce alcohol entirely. He will have to triple the amount of vegetables he is eating. He will need to do 30 minutes of exercise five days a week. And he will have to inject himself with a drug for the rest of his life at four-hour intervals throughout the day.

In this situation, the patient may make Appraisal 2b and decide that the behavioural modifications being asked of him are simply too harrowing. He has much lower self-efficacy. He doesn't believe that the change is going to be at all straightforward. He doubts his own willpower and tenacity.

And that's a major problem. The danger here is that, rather than tackling the threat of a heart attack itself, he may try to reduce the fear that he experiences. He may engage in psychological mechanisms such as denial (e.g. "I'm probably not as much at risk as the doctor says I am") or defensive avoidance (e.g. "This is all too scary so I'm not going to think about it any longer"). Another possible result may be aggressive reactance (e.g. "The doctor has a hidden agenda so I'm going to ignore this advice").

There are probably many reasons for the demise of once-prosperous Nokia and its subsequent takeover in 2014 by Microsoft. But through the lenses of these different fear appraisals, we can see why Stephen Elop's email to the Nokia workforce failed to have its intended effect.

Remember that, to be effective, a fear appeal has to pass successfully through two sets of filters. The first set is about the severity of the threat and people's perceived susceptibility to it. I'd say that Elop's letter does a reasonably good job of scaring his hapless employees – into forcing them to understand that the outlook is bleak (Appraisal 1a) and that they are all at risk (Appraisal 1b).

The second set of appraisals is about people's response efficacy and their self-efficacy. And it's here where we can see why Elop's email fails to do its job. Appraisal 2a asks, "Is it likely that a response on my part will tackle the root cause of the fear?" And the trouble was that his employees didn't know exactly what response they were being asked to follow. There was no clear command for how they should behave differently.

Without that clarity, the hapless employees within Nokia couldn't help but have low self-efficacy about their ability to perform the necessary behaviours to save the company. Elop talked about a burning oil platform, but I think that his email was more like a burning maze. It was scary but it afforded no solution. On the burning oil platform, it's clear that you need to jump into the swirling black seas below. But in a burning maze, what do you do? WHAT DO YOU DO?

It's like a doctor telling you that you have a bizarre and rare disease. You have the *Nimbulamus forivalis* virus. He shakes his head and sighs. And then, without any warning, he pushes you out of the door of the hospital without telling you what you're supposed to do to recover. You can see why the poor folks at Nokia weren't sure of the precise response – let alone whether it would work.

Designing effective fear appeals

Perhaps the most powerful emotion of all is the one that has been most deeply hard-wired into our psyches: fear. Kim Witte and fellow researcher Mike Allen from the University of Wisconsin-Milwaukee performed what's known as a meta-analysis of over 100 scientific studies looking at the effectiveness of different fear appeals on changing attitudes, intentions and behaviour. Based on this painstaking statistical examination of these many studies that have been conducted in countries all over the world, we know that effective fear appeals must satisfy four conditions:[11]

- **Severity of threat.** Appraisal 1a says that an audience must believe that the danger is sufficiently significant that it is genuinely worth avoiding. If the worst-case scenario of taking a new recreational drug is only a minor and temporary headache, that's hardly going to stop anyone. But if the risk is that you may end up bleeding uncontrollably from your eye sockets, that's clearly something much scarier. Health crusaders have found that using gruesome images (e.g. of what happens to a smoker's lungs or to drug addicts that end up dying in horrible circumstances) can magnify threat severity.
- **Susceptibility to the threat.** Appraisal 1b tells us that an audience must feel that they are personally likely to be affected by the threat. Just think about weather forecasts: people generally only care about forecasts for where they live. So if a situation only affects the sales department, clearly the rest of the organization isn't going to care. If a disease only affects women over the age of 40, everyone else will stop paying attention. If the probability of getting caught and prosecuted for tax evasion is tiny, most of the world may take their chances. The lesson: ensure that a fear appeal is targeted at the right section of people who feel personally susceptible.
- **High response efficacy.** Appraisal 2a suggests that an audience must believe that the proposed response will be beneficial. So consider how you will prove that taking action will neutralize the threat. Will your software definitely protect users' computers from viruses? Will getting a certain qualification massively reduce workers' chances

(Continued)

119

of getting made redundant from work? Is a vaccine definitely effective? If your proposed response isn't well known to people, think about using stories, examples, awards, scientific studies or other evidence to support your assertion that behaving in a certain way has a high chance of doing away with the threat.

- **High self-efficacy.** Finally, Appraisal 2b reminds us that the response must be easy to follow. An audience must believe that they will be able to follow the advice and that it won't be too taxing. This simply substantiates what we've all known for a long time: people are incorrigibly lazy. Yes, a threat may be significant (Appraisal 1a) and personally relevant (Appraisal 1b). But people often engage in denial or other psychological coping mechanisms to ignore or otherwise downplay threats rather than take action. If your proposed response is not simple then perhaps a fear appeal isn't the best way to go.

Remember that an effective fear appeal must satisfy *all* four appraisals. Anyone can scare an audience. But can you also help people believe that your solution will work (Appraisal 2a) and that they can apply your solution (Appraisal 2b), too? Those latter two appraisals are perhaps the more challenging bits to think about.

Fear appeals work, although I appreciate that the four appraisals don't make for easy reading. Terms such as "high response efficacy" and "susceptibility to the threat" don't exactly trip off the tongue. They aren't easy to remember. There's no snappy acronym that binds them together.

But hopefully you'll appreciate that this is what the science tells us. And you'd rather learn about something that works than something that's been dumbed down, right?

Perhaps one of the most successful fear campaigns of recent decades has been the one highlighting the risks of HIV and AIDS. When HIV was first discovered, there was no treatment. But for most people in the developed world, at least, the core part of the solution was fairly straightforward: wear a condom during sex.

Even though different countries around the world tailored the message in different ways, the central commandment was the same and fulfilled all four conditions. First, the threat was severe (Appraisal 1a). Back in the 1980s, infection with HIV led to AIDS, which led to death. There was no cure. Death was inevitable.

Every sexually active person was at risk too. It wasn't just an issue for one gender. It wasn't something that only hit older people or a particular ethnic group or individuals with certain sexual preferences. No, it was a danger to anyone and everybody who had sex with anyone else. So that ticked the box for Appraisal 1b.

But thankfully, prevention wasn't overly complicated either. Wearing a condom during sex was highly effective (Appraisal 2a). And it only took a little forethought to put into practice. It took relatively little effort to buy condoms and slip one on during sex (Appraisal 2b). As a result, people were successfully scared into action.

So remember both Nokia's failure and the **Fear appeals** condom campaign's triumph. It's fairly easy to **work.** scare people. But when it comes down to scaring them *into action*, we need to both raise their level of anxiety *and* give them a relatively clear-cut way of reducing it again.

Inspiring through high expectations

The early 1960s were a time of fear. At the height of the Cold War between the United States and the Soviet Union, many Americans were scared that the Soviets would ultimately win the space race. After all, the Soviets had already won a key stage of the contest by being the first nation to put their cosmonaut Yuri Gagarin into space.

In 1962, US president John F. Kennedy attempted to rally the nation with a big announcement. His ambition: to land an American on the moon. In a speech that electrified the 35,000 guests packing out a football stadium at Rice University in Texas, he proclaimed:

> We choose to go to the Moon. We choose to go to the Moon in this decade and do the other things not because they are easy, but because they are hard, because that goal will serve to organize and measure the best of our energies and skills, because that challenge is one that we are willing to accept, one we are unwilling to postpone, and one which we intend to win, and the others, too.

At that point, getting to the Moon was a gargantuan, almost unbelievably daunting scientific and engineering challenge. Orbiting the Earth as Yuri Gagarin had done meant being about 100 miles above the Earth's surface, but the Moon is over 238,000 miles further than that. That's like you having learnt a couple of dozen words of a new language such as Mandarin Chinese or Arabic and then deciding to master 57,000 more!

However, Kennedy's speech had its desired effect. And only seven years later, American astronaut Neil Armstrong was the first person to walk on the Moon.

To me, that's a pretty *wow* speech and a magnificent result.

Nowadays, the term "moon shot" is often used to describe those big bets, those inspiring, audacious goals that could make a massive difference. And University of Lausanne academics John

Antonakis, Marika Fenley and Sue Liechti found that setting high expectations is yet another way in which we can coax and win audiences over.[12]

By training people in the application of techniques such as the setting of high expectations, the researchers were able to burnish their charisma in measurable ways. It made audiences sit up, take notice and *want* to hear more.

You're probably familiar with the notion of organizational vision, which is really just another way of saying that a leader has a set of high expectations for a group. For example, the online retail giant Amazon describes its vision thus: "Amazon.com strives to be Earth's most customer-centric company where people can find and discover virtually anything they want to buy online."[13]

Or consider the vision statement of the British broadcaster the BBC. In a single sentence, its purpose is: "To be the most creative organization in the world."

Neither Amazon nor the BBC wants to be *one* of the best. Amazon yearns to be *Earth's* most customer-centric company. The BBC seeks to be the most innovative organization in the *world*. If those aren't high expectations, I don't know what are.

A vision should be an inspiring, vivid picture of a possible future – as a means of igniting people's imaginations and stirring them to action. Such pronouncements aren't only made up of numbers or financial targets but paint a rich portrait of what's possible. But clearly, visions are merely examples of attempts to inspire through high expectations.

Personally, I think the concept of a vision is somewhat limiting. Vision tends to have quite specific connotations and can be a bit off-putting: many folks think of it as something that only leaders or politicians can use in reference to the future of a business, a charity, a government agency or an entire country.

Setting specific, difficult goals consistently leads to a greater upswing in performance. But *anyone* can set high expectations. You don't have to be a leader. You don't have to have any formal authority at all.

You could be a parent wanting more from your family. You could be a member of a community seeking to clean up your part of town. You could be a relatively lowly employee urging your workmates to cut costs so that management doesn't have to cut jobs. You could be a football player wanting to motivate your teammates to train harder and win the local league.

I think of high expectations as a more useful term, liberated from the jargon-y undertone of vision and the suggestion that you need to be the boss. So don't worry about grand visions. Set high expectations for people instead.

It will work too. A sizeable body of research suggests that setting specific, difficult goals consistently leads to a greater upswing in performance than merely urging individuals to do their best. Or, as the highly decorated psychologists Edwin Locke and Gary Latham write in a review of 35 years of studies into goal setting: "When people are asked to do their best, they do not do so."[14] It takes that bigger goal to get the best out of people.

So try it the next time you're attempting to spur people into action. If you set a stretching, audacious goal for your workmates, family, community or whatever, they may just achieve it. But aim for mediocrity and you'll never get more than middling performance in return.

There's a slight wrinkle, though. It's not enough simply to set a stretching goal. It's actually just part one of a two-stage process.

124

To explain further, let me introduce the popular, cheesy saying: "If you believe, you can achieve." A quick search on Google threw up 178,000,000 hits for this popular aphorism. I generally dislike such trite claims. But research tells me that I shouldn't be quite so dismissive on this occasion.

It's not enough simply to set a stretching goal. It's actually just part one of a two-stage process.

There's a mass of scientific evidence suggesting that people's self-efficacy – or their belief that they can successfully do what's necessary to achieve a given result – can affect their actual performance on a task. Even if two individuals have similar levels of finesse and experience at a task, it's likely that the one with greater self-efficacy will end up performing better.

Think about sporting champions in almost any discipline. It could be in an individual sport such as golf or a team sport such as football. Often, sporting heroes and heroines have access to pretty much the same training and resources as their competitors. They may have no greater physical advantages. So what is it that helps them succeed? Their self-belief, their conviction that they can win through: their self-efficacy.

The same is true of teams in the workplace, community groups and other gatherings of people. A business unit's team-efficacy or a group's collective-efficacy can determine their performance. For example, one study led by Abhishek Srivastava at West Virginia University looked at the beliefs of management teams across a chain of 102 hotels in the United States. Results showed that the teams' beliefs in their ability to hit hotel targets – for example measured by their level of agreement with the phrase "We are confident of achieving the occupancy goal of our hotel" – was able to predict their actual performance. Teams that had higher levels of efficacy achieved better results.[15]

How do you boost people's self-efficacy? You can train them so that they actually have better skills. You can also show them examples of others performing the same or similar tasks so that they feel more equipped to do so. But you can also stoke their confidence through the words you use. You can tell people that you believe utterly in their ability to perform well.

And it will work. In the words of Albert Bandura, one of the true godfathers of psychological science: "people who are socially persuaded that they possess the capabilities to master difficult situations ... are likely to mobilize greater effort."[16]

Consider the chief operating officer at a flourishing online business that I've been working with for a couple of years. After a major software problem and the hard-hitting loss of their biggest customer, he prepared a short speech to give at a hastily called company-wide meeting.

I watched him say: "We've taken a major blow, but it's like one of those action movies when the hero has been badly beaten. He's down but we know he'll save the day. We may be down but we're not defeated. I can honestly say that this room is filled with the most talented people I have ever worked with. I believe wholeheartedly that we can recover and learn from this situation. I would bet you any amount of money that we will look back on this in six months' time as nothing more than a blip."

Tell people that you believe utterly in their ability to perform well.

Sometimes people need to have faith that they can achieve what they have been tasked with doing. For employees, a family or a community to believe in themselves, they sometimes need someone else to believe in them first.

Helping others to reach your high expectations

By all means set high expectations. But make sure you also instil in your audience a belief that the goal can actually be achieved.

It's fine if you have the size and resources of Amazon or the BBC to say that you wish to be the most customer-centric or creative organization on the planet. But is that realistic for a three-person start-up?

High expectations have to be stretching but not unthinkable. Arduous but just about achievable.

Equally as important, though, you have to boost people's self-efficacy – their belief in their ability to succeed. One of the best ways: remind them of times in the past when they succeeded. Ask people to talk you through similar challenges they faced and overcame. Or repeat their accomplishments back to them if you know them well enough.

If you know people well, you can repeat back to them what you know of the experience that they have, their skills, their courage, their intelligence or their determination. Give them examples of how other similar individuals confronted comparable challenges and succeeded too.

Be inspirational and uplifting and people may eke out that extra little bit of effort. Convince them that you truly believe in their ability to achieve and they may just do so.

Using metaphor, simile and analogy

Six months ago, I coached an individual who was struggling to network more effectively. He's a musician, songwriter and music producer who had some early success but has of late fallen into a rut. He felt he wasn't getting the kind of high-profile work he wanted; he realized that he probably hadn't made enough effort to network and make himself known to the right people.

But he faltered at the idea. He didn't feel he could do it.

During one of our regular coaching sessions, I tried to explain networking to him differently. I suggested that networking is just like songwriting. Each fresh song (like every networking meeting) may be different. But the more you write (or network with new faces), the more able you become to recognize patterns of notes (or patterns of conversation). So you get faster at assembling new clusters of words and notes (or better at networking with different people).

And that put his mind at rest. By explaining networking in a different fashion – in terms that took into account his very specific background – he felt much more confident to get out there and network more.

Not many months later, he described his newfound confidence when it came to networking. In an email, he wrote: "I've been pushing myself, engineering meetings, growing my little black book, and maybe quite enjoying it. I've had a slight mind-shift, a minor epiphany by which I mean that beforehand I understood networking but only conceptually. Now I understand more practically and with greater depth."

Studies tell us that using analogies, similes and metaphors helps us to be more beguiling, to be more impactful. For instance, Annette Towler at the University of Colorado trained a group of experimental participants in the application of charismatic influencing techniques which included using metaphors and analogies. When she asked audiences to judge presentations given by these participants, she found that these participants outperformed another group of control participants who had been trained merely in standard presentation skills, i.e. in the use of physical gestures, facial expressions and eye contact.[17]

Before we go on though, I have to admit to a slight problem. I often get metaphors, similes and analogies tangled up. In case you're like me, I thought I'd include dictionary definitions and examples of all three.

Using analogies, similes and metaphors helps us to be more memorable.

Metaphor (noun)

1. A figure of speech in which a term or phrase is applied to something to which it is not literally applicable in order to suggest a connection.
2. A figure of speech containing an implied comparison.
   Examples: "Our words are weapons against ignorance." "We live life in the fast lane and it's only getting faster." "These funds will form a safety net for those who are struggling." "We stand on the shoulders of those who went before us."

Simile (noun)

1. A figure of speech involving comparison of one thing with another thing of a different kind.
2. A figure of speech in which two dissimilar things are explicitly compared, often using the word "like" or "as".
   Examples: "Life is like a box of chocolates." "You must be as courageous as a lion." "The idea is as clear as mud." "Leading a group of creative people is as straightforward as trying to herd bees."

Analogy (noun)

1. A comparison between one thing and another made for the purpose of explanation or clarification.
2. A method of explaining an idea by referring to a similar or more familiar idea.

   Examples: "Business is like poker. Whoever shows their hand first is the one to lose." "Short-term memory is like your computer's RAM, while long-term memory is more like the hard drive." "We must treat customers more like hand-made cupcakes than sausages that we pump out of a machine."

Actually, I don't think that the precise meanings of the three matter when it comes to being captivating and spellbinding. The point isn't about distinguishing them but *using* them – *including* them in our speeches and conversations.

Further evidence about their power comes again from the analysis of renowned speeches. When researchers led by Cynthia Emrich at Purdue University dissected speeches given by US presidents, they found that presidents who used more image-based rhetoric in their inaugural addresses were generally judged to be more charismatic.[18] By using words and phrases that evoked images, sounds, smells and feelings, they were more able to influence and win over the people around them.

Take President Barack Obama's 2013 inaugural address, for example.[19] Read a transcript or listen to him speaking and you'll hear phrases like "We believe that America's prosperity must rest upon the broad shoulders of a rising middle class."

Clearly, he wasn't referring to anyone's actual shoulders. But he created a visual image that called to America's growing middle class through his use of metaphor.

Some further examples from the same speech:

- "The American people can no more meet the demands of today's world by acting alone than American soldiers could have met the forces of fascism or communism with muskets and militias." (Analogy)
- "America will remain the anchor of strong alliances in every corner of the globe." (Metaphor)
- "With common effort and common purpose, with passion and dedication, let us answer the call of history and carry into an uncertain future that precious light of freedom." (Metaphor)

Written down, such metaphors and analogies can appear rather tame and uninspiring. But it turns out that metaphors in particular have intriguing effects within our brains.

We know this conclusively because of a 2014 paper in the *Journal of Cognitive Neuroscience* written by language and emotion aficionados Francesca Citron from the Free University of Berlin and Adele Goldberg from Princeton University. The objective of their study: to compare the effects of metaphorical versus literal language on brain activity.

The researchers invited participants to read a variety of sentences while having the blood flow in their brains scanned by magnetic resonance imaging (MRI) machines. Some of the sentences were literal (e.g. "She looked at him kindly" and "He had a nasty personality"), while others had almost identical meanings but used metaphors instead (e.g. "She looked at him sweetly" and "He had a bitter personality").

The scientists noticed distinct patterns of cerebral activation. The metaphors activated more areas of brain circuitry, in particular the amygdala and the anterior portion of the hippocampus, both of which are associated with the processing of emotion. In other words, the metaphorical expressions were more emotionally engaging than their literal counterparts.

Metaphors in particular have intriguing effects within our brains.

What's more, the research team noted that they had picked fairly conventional metaphorical expressions rather than creating new and obscure ones. So it seems that even fairly unoriginal metaphors may stimulate more chunks of grey matter than their more literal equivalents.[20]

The takeaway: if you want to make an impact, deploy the occasional metaphor. Do so and your words may soar.

Using metaphor for maximal persuasion

A couple of studies have looked specifically at the conditions that help maximize the persuasive effects of metaphor. Some advice:

- **Use metaphors that resonate with your audience.** One study tried to change the attitudes of different audiences by using a sports metaphor. Those in the audience who were sports fans were more impressed by the arguments; those who weren't sports fans were actually less persuaded. So make sure you use metaphors that make sense – or resonate – with your audience. Again, this finding is really affirming what we established earlier on in this chapter: understand your audience's particular background first.
- **Introduce your metaphor early.** Reviewing a large collection of studies looking at the advantage of metaphorical over literal language, communication researchers Pradeep Sopory and James Dillard found that metaphors were most effective when used early in a speech.[21] Their analysis doesn't tell us why. I could speculate that it's because audiences are more alert earlier on and more likely to drift off in the latter sections of a speech or presentation – but I really am only guessing. Anyway, the moral: don't allow your beautifully constructed metaphor to go to waste in the hinterlands of your address or lecture.

Images can be metaphors too. Consider the iceberg slide that I described in the Introduction. It's a visual metaphor I've been using for a long time to great success. When I say at workshops and seminars that presence and charisma are only the tip of the iceberg, I don't mean that literally. But it's an elegant way to illustrate that there's a lot that goes on within most people that can't be seen just by meeting them.

I shall leave you with one final example. I attended a conference some months ago at around the same time as I started reviewing research papers on the topic of symbolic language. The chief technology officer of a blossoming software firm was speaking about the difficulty of developing new products. He said: "Progress does not march forward like an army on parade. It crawls back and forth, sideways and turning on its belly like a guerrilla."

I thought it was an evocative image painted with words. To suggest that progress is not something that occurs in an orderly fashion but is won gradually through fits and starts, with apparent missteps and changes of direction.

And on that note, let's change direction by looking at a completely different device for standing out from the crowd.

Invoking moral arguments

"What's in it for me?"

It's a question that is quoted so frequently on sales training courses that it even has its own acronym: WIIFM.

But it's often excellent advice. Ask anyone to do something differently and it's often worth imagining that your audience has asked this question. Why should anyone do as you say? What's in it for them?

WIIFM is about enticing audiences to behave differently by appealing to their self-interest. If you want to sell a product or service, it's worth running through the benefits to customers, clients or consumers. These may include personal gains, such as profit, status and prestige; greater convenience; less pain or stress; more pleasure; lower costs and so on.

However, we can also inspire audiences to modify their ways by doing precisely the opposite. Rather than speak to their selfishness, we can appeal to their self*less*ness.

Try to shift people's focus towards moral concerns about making a contribution to something bigger. Moral statements are announcements aimed at motivating an audience to do the right thing – to be decent or even virtuous. They appeal to people's higher sense of ethics and honour. And they work because, according to social psychologist Boas Shamir at the Hebrew University in Israel, "A sense of moral correctness is a source of strength and confidence. Having complete faith in the moral correctness of one's convictions gives one the strength and confidence to behave accordingly."[22]

So consider tapping into that source of strength and confidence. Try to shift people's focus away from their personal interests and towards moral concerns about making a contribution to something bigger.

Of course, this is something that charities have to do all the time. An example: not long ago, I started working with Andrew Berwick, chief executive of the Access Project, a charity aiming to help disadvantaged school kids improve their grades so they can get into top universities.

"To fund the programme, we find businesses who will partner with our schools. It involves a financial commitment as well as a commitment to encourage staff to volunteer to tutor kids one on one," Berwick told me.

The 30-year-old comes across as a steely leader, an impression perhaps furthered by a shaved head and a tendency to express his emotions through guarded, tight-lipped smiles. Having left the data-driven world of management consulting to take the helm of the charity, his early approach to persuading businesses to get involved was to focus on the problem. Armed with a presentation full of statistics, he wanted to impress upon potential business partners that many socially disadvantaged children across the country were being hampered in not only their academic ambitions but ultimately also their chances in life.

"Unfortunately, it didn't work so well. People did not want to hear about the scale of the problem. They already knew the problem," he added.

In other words, he discovered that it simply wasn't necessary to hammer home the point about social disadvantage. The business people he spoke to already understood the need. They already felt obligated to do something. All they needed was to ensure that Berwick and his charity were an effective solution: that he and the Access Project could actually deliver real opportunities for disadvantaged teens.

Moral statements aren't about arguing in terms of costs and benefits. They are not about profit and loss or other tangible consequences. They tap into some of our most deep-seated emotions; we all desire to be altruistic, generous, caring, noble, helpful individuals.

We all desire to be altruistic, generous, caring, noble, helpful individuals.

But it's not only charities that can tap into moral arguments. Day to day, we all want to

135

feel as if we're useful, that we're being helpful to those around us – even if they are strangers. For instance, I recently listened to Paula O'Connor, a contact centre manager, trying to rally her team to deliver better customer service: "Doing well by our customers isn't something that we do only because it's our job. Imagine that it's the family and friends of people you know on the other end of the phone. Imagine it's your best mate's uncle or grandmother. You'd want to do well by them, wouldn't you?"

To sum up: yes, audiences often do act purely in their own grubby self-interest. But they can be persuaded to behave differently for the greater good too. And moral statements are your tool for tapping into that vein of selflessness.

Crafting moral statements

Jonathan Haidt, a professor of social psychology at the University of Virginia and a respected authority on moral behaviour, suggests that there are at least five broad categories of morals:[23]

- **Care and altruism for others:** wanting to do well by others, e.g. vulnerable individuals who need protection from harm.
- **Fairness, reciprocity, justice and equality:** ensuring that everyone in society is treated a certain way and has access to the same social and physical resources.
- **Loyalty to a group:** demonstrating self-sacrifice and putting the needs of your family, community or even nation first.
- **Respect for tradition and authority:** demonstrating deference to more senior people so long as they have legitimate sources of expertise, authorization or clout.
- **Belief in purity or sanctity of the human body:** in practice this often means avoiding disgusting or degrading situations, actions or ideas.

In questioning people from all over the world, Haidt has found that these moral categories seem true for different cultures just about everywhere on the planet. So how could you appeal to the higher values of an audience to drive the kinds of change in attitude or behaviour that you're looking for?

Telling tales

Step into RADA Studios in central London and you may be within touching distance of a future superstar. The Royal Academy of Dramatic Art has birthed theatrical and film actors including Anthony Hopkins, Diana Rigg and Clive Owen.

But back to business. Last summer, I was there for thefuturestory, a seminar run by communications agency theblueballroom. And yes, they don't seem to like capitalization or even spaces between words!

Billed as an opportunity to hear speakers and panellists discuss the topic of data, we in the audience were educated about the differences between big data, open data and personal data. We were told about an imminent wave of European legislation around data protection that would force organizations to treat customer data with greater sensitivity. We learnt that not all data is created equally but can be rated based on properties such as velocity, veracity and value. At times, the debate descended into geekspeak with terminology such as *semantic* data versus *normalized* data, which were comprehensible only to a handful of people apart from the expert panellists themselves.

Before such discussions, though, a diminutive woman with coiffed blonde hair and glasses had kicked the day off. Approaching a lectern in front of the audience, she introduced herself as Sheila Parry, founder and managing director of theblueballroom. Then, speaking with the warmth of a kindly schoolteacher, she launched into a story.

Parry had recently been engrossed by a biography of Alan Turing, the legendary code breaker and perhaps the father of modern day computer science. His greatest achievement: leading the effort that successfully cracked Nazi Germany's secret Enigma code and arguably ended World War II several years early.

Telling a story is fundamental to making subjects more tangible and interesting

But she shared with us her dismay on learning that Turing – probably one of the most brilliant minds of the 20th century – suffered the ignominy of being prosecuted by the British establishment for gross indecency. Why? Because he was a homosexual and his very existence was considered criminal by the draconian laws of 1952. Two years later, he was found dead from cyanide poisoning, which may have been suicide or a wretched accident.

Parry carried on by telling us about Turing's childhood, about his achievements as an athlete at school. We in the audience learnt of the awkward relationship he had had with his mother, too.

But years before his fall from favour, Turing had devised an Automatic Computer Engine, a forerunner to today's computers. On unveiling the machine to the world in 1946, a newspaper journalist asked whether such computers might one day be able to play chess.

Turing's answer: that it might be possible, in a hundred years' time.

The audience – myself included – chuckled as Parry recounted Turing's stupendously inaccurate prediction. Of course, computer science has moved on rather considerably since then.

Essentially, the punchline to Parry's story can be summarized in a single sentence: that technology transforms the world very quickly and in ways we often can't predict. But why did she take 10 minutes to tell the story of her personal discovery of Alan Turing's life?

"The idea of telling a story is fundamental to making subjects that are often very abstract more tangible and interesting," Parry told me some weeks later.

One on one, she struck me as somebody with deep reservoirs of empathy and concern for other people, the sort of person who seeks to do right by her employees and clients even if there may occasionally be a cost to herself.

"I wanted to make connections between things that were considered irrelevant, historic and in the past with the ideas of invention and innovation. I wanted to share the story with people to excite them about data and technology and the idea of digital analytics. Otherwise, their eyes would glaze over."

In other words, her epiphany was that the topic of data might appear academic or even irrelevant to attendees at the event. So she set about humanizing the subject by sharing Alan Turing's exploits.

Strictly speaking, Parry could have left out the details of his personal life and tragic end. But she left them in because it brought his story to life. She made us feel for the brilliant but mistreated Alan Turing and in turn to care about the human side of data. She moved us to take an interest in an area which might otherwise have been esoteric and technically complicated.

Story can be a powerful placeholder, a way of bringing even the most obscure subject matter to life. And that's not just an assertion either: when it comes to changing minds, multiple studies tell us that stories and anecdotes often beat carefully assembled statistics.[24]

Story can be a powerful placeholder, a way of bringing even the most obscure subject matter to life.

As just one example, consider a study conducted by a clutch of business and management scholars led by economist Michal Herzenstein at the University of Delaware. The researchers wanted to explore the factors that helped business owners borrow money on prosper.com, a peer-to-peer lending website.[25]

The notion behind peer-to-peer lending is that entrepreneurs can post listings online asking for money. Private individuals such as you or I read those listings and then can decide to lend them money in exchange for fixed monthly payments.

It can be an excellent way for borrowers to raise funds without having to submit heaps of paperwork to banks. Investors too can sometimes get better returns than they would otherwise get from investing in a straightforward savings account.

But there are no guarantees. Borrowers sometimes default on their payments. If they go bust or simply abscond with the funds, investors may end up losing out. So there are risks as well as returns for investors.

Anyway, back to the study. Herzenstein and her colleagues noticed that borrowers could write a paragraph about themselves. For example, a business owner could talk about how he struggled with poverty early on in life but, owing to the kindness of others, developed a fierce determination to succeed. Another borrower could speak of her hopes for her family and her community and how her unshakeable religious beliefs meant that she was a safe investment. But because business owners and investors never meet, such sob stories are pretty much unverifiable statements. They may have been true. Then again, they may have been delusions or outright lies.

But it didn't matter. The researchers found that borrowers who wrote such narratives about their past experiences, current circumstances or **Stories are a marketing tool.** future hopes were statistically more likely to get funded. In other words, borrowers who told stories were more successful in getting money from lenders.

The conclusion reached by the economists was so clear that they titled their paper: "Tell me a good story and I may lend you my money." All of humanity – you and I and everybody else – is influenced by stories.

A final observation: that their paper was published in the *Journal of Marketing Research* says something too. Essentially, stories are a marketing tool, a method for increasing the persuasiveness of whatever message a storyteller is pushing.

A story is like a persuasion bullet being fired deep into the brain. Tell more stories.

Using stories to sway your audience

Novices often pack their presentations or pitches with facts and figures. But more seasoned folks know that there are few conversations, lectures or presentations that can't be made more entertaining, accessible and memorable with the aid of a story or two.

To what extent do you tell stories? When you're trying to cajole a loved one to lose weight, you could tell inspirational stories

(Continued)

of how others have lost weight and benefited. If you're attempting to sell a product, perhaps impart an anecdote about how another customer used it and loved it. Your story could be about an incompetent politician aimed at making people furious enough to want to oust him.

But stories don't just have to be tales of actual events. Consider using hypothetical stories, myths and fables to get audiences to listen too. When you're next trying to win someone or a group over, what story could you use to change pace and make them sit up and take notice?

If you previously read my book *How To Win: The Argument, the Pitch, the Job, the Race* (Capstone), you'll know that I talk about storytelling in that book too. Why am I mentioning it again?

Because in the two years since I wrote it, I'm *still* seeing too many speakers rely on facts and figures. I still hear too few stories. So forgive me if you already read that book. But until the *majority* of

I still hear too few stories.

people are using stories to win hearts and minds, I'll keep making this point: *tell more stories.*

Sharing your autobiographical adventures

Parry's story about Alan Turing was clearly about someone other than her. But autobiographical stories – stories about ourselves – may be an even more potent device for persuasion.

I ate some rather tasty marshmallows recently. And it led to me discovering an interesting personal story.

142

But first, the marshmallows. Most are white or pink and are spongy, fairly insubstantial and very sweet. You can't really say that they taste of much.

Until I tried a raspberry marshmallow with enough actual raspberries in it to hint at the real thing – raspberry pips even got stuck in my teeth. There was a cappuccino marshmallow that delivered an espresso kick. A mint and dark chocolate marshmallow was studded with chunks of real chocolate.

These grown-up marshmallows are the brainchild of Harriot Pleydell-Bouverie, founder of buzzy start-up Mallow & Marsh. And I learnt that her tale was perhaps her greatest marketing weapon.

"I started my company backwards," she told me.

Pleydell-Bouverie has a fresh face, dark eyes and long dark hair that you could imagine being featured in a TV commercial for a hair styling product. But she speaks with an energy that hints that she is not to be underestimated.

She didn't strategically analyse the market and decide on the optimal product to launch. In fact, she stumbled quite accidentally into making marshmallows.

Back in 2012, the then 27-year-old had set up an online jewellery boutique. While attending a weekend workshop for entrepreneurs wanting to grow their businesses, one of her fellow moguls-in-the-making challenged her to make a batch of marshmallows.

Stories about ourselves may be an even more potent device for persuasion.

"Someone bet me that I couldn't make marshmallows at home. I really knew nothing about marshmallows but loved to cook and thought I'd give it a go," she said.

Handing out the marshmallows the next day was a life-changing moment.

"The reaction was incredible. I had literally never seen a reaction like this. Everyone loved them and the intrigue around the marshmallows was infectious," she laughed.

Her jewellery business was not gaining much traction. So it was an easy decision to pivot from one to the other.

"With my marshmallows, I just threw myself into it. I was a one-person business who didn't over-plan. I just created a product, tested it quickly and easily at market stalls and developed it from there," added Pleydell-Bouverie.

She promptly landed a distribution deal with a major supermarket chain. She has won a legion of loyal, gourmet-food-appreciating fans too.

At least part of the brand's appeal is Pleydell-Bouverie's story. The fact that she fell into her business concept, that she's a budding entrepreneur striving to take on the confectionary multinationals and grow a business single-handedly.

Clearly, the taste of the product, its uniqueness, helps to drive sales. But would the business have grown so quickly if the marshmallows had been developed in the test kitchens of a soulless conglomerate? Probably not.

"People love my story. They love an underdog. I've got the jewellery business that failed and I shout about it. I'm proud of that. I call it my MBA for entrepreneurs and it's where I learnt all my mistakes."

Yes, autobiographical stories can be incredibly persuasive. But even Pleydell-Bouverie admits that they are not appropriate in every context.

She made this discovery in her conversations with customers as opposed to consumers. Her consumers are the supermarket shoppers buying a pack or handful of packs of her marshmallows – and they tend to love her story. But she also has to sell to customers, those professional buyers who decide what to order onto supermarket shelves.

"Buyers have different agendas because their concerns are price-related or category-related," she explained. **Stories are not appropriate in every context.**

As such, professional buyers are at best only tangentially interested or entirely immune to her story. For them, a fact-laden presentation may actually be the better bet.

So autobiographical stories *can* be – in many, but not all situations – a powerful tool. That's as true whether you're entertaining friends or raising funds at a charity dinner. But hopefully by now you aren't wondering *whether* to tell stories but *which* stories about yourself to recount.

Telling autobiographical tales

We've already established that stories help to set you apart from the competition. Clearly, autobiography is a kind of story. But it's not just any story. It's your story – it's your personal connection to a topic.

Why are you fired up about the issue or idea that you're discussing? Is it something that affected you when you were growing up or something that dawned on you more recently?

If you're promoting a product or service, consider discussing your personal experience of it. Maybe you benefited when you

(Continued)

145

discovered it – or struggled and lost out precisely because you didn't have access to it.

I want to emphasize that autobiographical stories are worth telling. Sometimes there is a perception in the world of work that there should be a partition keeping the professional and the personal apart. That work should be about facts, projections, statistics and logic, that there is no place for idiosyncratic stories, feelings and personal anecdotes.

But that's emphatically not true. Even captains of industry and political leaders are as influenced by stories as the rest of us. So please do consider sharing your personal story too.

Using contrasts and lists

Dozens if not hundreds of studies are conducted every year looking at what helps superstars connect with audiences and communicate so resoundingly. And one of the most high-profile strands of research focuses on speeches given by celebrated political figures such as Winston Churchill, Martin Luther King and John F. Kennedy to see what patterns they can discern. We've already encountered a couple of such studies in this chapter.

But Dutch scholars Deanne Den Hartog and Robert Verburg at VU Amsterdam took a different approach by analysing prominent speeches of international business leaders, including the late Anita Roddick of the Body Shop in the UK and Jan Timmer of Dutch electronics business Philips. Their perhaps surprising conclusion: "The most widely used resource of orators is probably the contrast."[26]

Let's consider an example. Anita Roddick once argued in front of the International Chamber of Commerce in Mexico: "Remember, corporations are invented. They are human institutions, not species found in nature."

A contrast is merely a statement in which you mention one thing as well as its direct opposite. In Roddick's speech, the word "not" clearly juxtaposes the ideas of human institutions with species found in nature.

Consider another example from a more literary source. Nobel and Pulitzer prize-winning author John Steinbeck once wrote in his book *Travels with Charley*: "What good is the warmth of summer, without the cold of winter to give it sweetness."

By setting something in opposition to its counterpart, we can emphasize the choices on offer or perhaps the consequences of not pursuing a course of action. Some further examples:

- "Carry on living a humdrum life or choose now to experience excitement along the way."
- "We have the opportunity to do either immense good or great evil."
- "Either we succeed brilliantly or fail miserably."
- "Great salespeople are not born. They are forged through hard work."

As with metaphor, contrast is a purely stylistic tool. It adds very little in terms of pure information. But discussing one idea and then pointing to its starkest opposite can give your words added weight.

> A contrast is a statement in which you mention one thing as well as its direct opposite.

Moving on, the Dutch researchers also suggest, "Another rhetorical device, which is almost as effective and popular as the contrast, is the three-part list."

147

Why a three-part list? Den Hartog and Verburg argue, "three is both the minimal number to unambiguously establish a connection and the maximally economic number for doing so without being excessive."

A three-part list is merely a catalogue of lessons, sound bites or messages to take away. Some examples:

- "We have the best product, the brightest people and a breathtaking opportunity before us."
- "There are three actions you need to do: cut down on salt, eat less red meat and drink less alcohol. Salt, red meat, alcohol."
- "As I scan the room, I see our extraordinary past, our difficult present and our ambitious future gathered around me."
- "Selling to customers is about empathy, empathy, empathy."

A three-part list is merely a catalogue of lessons, sound bites or messages.

Personally, I think it's a bit restrictive to use only three-part lists. Effective lists can sometimes stretch to four or even five items, especially if they are bound together by a common thread. For example, I once heard a chief executive warn his business: "The four horsemen of this company's impending Apocalypse are: complacency, customer apathy, cash flow and conflict between departments."

Clearly, that's four problems rather than a mere three. But it made for a superb statement. And you'll notice that the list was doubly powerful because it featured alliteration by the repeated use of the letter 'c' in the four items too.

I personally get a big kick out of creating acronyms – using the letters of a three-, four- or five-letter word to spell out a list or sequence. For instance, I suggest in my previous book *How To Win: The Argument, the Pitch, the Job, the Race* that speakers should

148

SOAR in order to tell compelling stories. The letters hopefully help would-be storytellers to compose engaging, complete tales by paying attention to what is really just a four-part list:

- Situation
- Obstacles
- Actions
- Result.

Perhaps you're thinking that contrasts and lists sound too easy, too obvious to have any true impact. After all, it's hardly difficult to write a contrast. Simply take two things that are opposites and shove them in the same sentence. A list is even easier: just mention three, four or more things in the same sentence. It's hardly rocket science.

Why, then, are contrasts and lists mentioned time and again in studies of great orators and authors? What makes a contrast or list truly memorable?

This was the quandary that British sociologists John Heritage and David Greatbatch at the University of Warwick set out to answer. To judge what made for a successful contrast or list versus an unsuccessful one, they decided to analyse recordings of real speeches made by politicians. Cunningly, they counted a contrast or list as successful only when it got a round of applause from the audience.[27]

To begin with, the instigators of this study looked at transcripts and watched video recordings of 476 political speeches delivered by British politicians. First of all, that's a lot of hot air to sit through, so the research duo should probably be congratulated for that fact alone.

Heritage and Greatbatch coded every sentence based on the presence of up to five separate nonverbal cues:

1. The speaker was gazing at the audience.

2. The sentence was delivered more loudly than the surrounding speech passage.
3. The sentence was spoken with a marked speeding up, slowing down or some other shift in rhythm.
4. The sentence was delivered with either greater pitch or stress variation.
5. The sentence was accompanied by the use of gestures.

A sentence with none of these features was classified as low impact. A sentence spoken with one feature was categorized as intermediate impact and sentences spoken with two or more features was tagged as high impact.

If you're thinking that this system of categorizing nonverbal cues looks familiar, you would be right. We came across an almost identical scheme back in Chapter 2, when we discussed a study also conducted by David Greatbatch but with a different research collaborator.

Looking at the contrasts that resulted in a round of applause, Heritage and Greatbatch discovered a clear pattern:

	Low impact	Intermediate impact	High impact
Percentage of contrasts that led to applause	5.1	29.8	45.4

As you can see, contrasts delivered in the total absence of nonverbal cues only triggered applause a meagre 5.1 per cent of the time. But the high impact contrasts delivered using two or more nonverbal cues led to applause 45.4 per cent of the time.

The importance of nonverbal cues on whether lists led to a round of applause was even more staggering:

	Low impact	Intermediate impact	High impact
Percentage of lists that led to applause	4.0	10.0	71.4

When a list was delivered without any nonverbal cues to make it more interesting, it also hardly ever led to a round of applause. Remember that the speeches that were analysed were delivered by politicians, so it's very likely that many – if not all – of these speeches were written by or at least had input from professional speech writers. But even the most judiciously constructed lists fell flat when delivered without accompanying nonverbal cues.

However, a humongous 71.4 per cent of lists led to applause when delivered in a high impact style. In other words, at least two non-verbal cues had to be used in conjunction with the list.

To me, the results of the analysis have two major implications.

First of all, it confirms that contrasts and lists *can* be highly effective rhetorical devices. They can be a way of crafting a memorable sound bite. However, the bigger lesson is that they need to be delivered in a nonverbally engrossing manner. It's not just about what you say. It's how you say it *as well*.

Consider an example of a list highlighted by the social scientists. The outspoken conservative politician Norman Tebbit intoned: "But in the winter of discontent, how many of the old, the sick, the unemployed, the disabled were bashed by unions?"

It's not just about what you say. It's how you say it *as well*.

Clearly, that list mentions four groups which have allegedly been victimized. On paper, it hardly looks remarkable – let alone something worthy of voracious applause. But it's *how* he said it that got a response from the audience.

Imagine that it's you who has to deliver the sentence. How would you say it? To make a point, I'd probably think about the cadence of the sentence. I'd stress certain words and use pauses. So I might say: "But in the winter of discontent [pause], how many of the *old* [pause], the *sick* [pause], the *unemployed* [pause], the *disabled* [pause] were *bashed* by unions." To punctuate things further, you might bring your hand down in a chopping motion or brandish a fist at the mention of each of the four disadvantaged groups.

There isn't a single right answer when it comes to choosing effective nonverbal delivery. But the point is to remember that people don't just listen to your words. They observe your whole performance.

Using contrasts and lists to hammer your point home

Rhetorical devices such as contrasts and lists aren't meant to be introduced merely for their own sake. You won't be more compelling or persuasive simply by dropping a bunch of them into your next speech or conversation.

Your aim is to use them to stress your key point or points. So what exactly is the core of your message?

Rather than using multiple contrasts and risk confusing an audience, I recommend constructing just one really strong contrast. So what is the single most critical choice, gap or distinction to which you wish to draw attention?

To keep matters simple, I'd utilize just one list, too. But consider repeating it enough times that it sticks in people's minds.

Perhaps introduce your list or acronym early on, talk through the individual items on the list and finally recap by referring back to it again.

Most importantly, remember that contrasts and lists have to be combined with sturdy nonverbal delivery to make them memorable. So think about your eye contact, stressing particular syllables, speaking more loudly – or softly – and so on.

Asking questions

So far we've discussed a handful of rhetorical techniques that can make us more charismatic, noteworthy and hopefully persuasive. For example, we learnt that even using a single, perspicaciously chosen metaphor may be enough to help our words soar. We discovered that emotions – both positive ones such as pride or exuberance as well as negative ones such as shame or fear – can bolster the effectiveness of our appeals. Even humble contrasts and lists may help to make our messages more captivating.

But before we go on, allow me to ask you a question. How likely is it that you will apply any of the techniques we've covered within the next two weeks?

If you want, you could answer the question by thinking of a percentage likelihood. So 0 per cent means there's no chance you will apply what we've discussed. And 100 per cent means you're so completely certain you will use them that you would be willing to give away your home and first-born child if you don't.

OK, so you have a percentage figure in mind. But it actually doesn't matter what figure you came up with. Because, believe it or not, simply by mulling over that question you will already be more likely to apply the techniques that we've covered.

Ask questions and you may influence real behaviour. We know this because of an ingenious study devised by researchers Jonathan Levav at Columbia University and Gavan Fitzsimons at Duke University. The investigative duo split a class of 145 MBA students into three randomly determined groups. Each group was asked to weigh up a different question:

- The first group was asked to estimate how likely they were to read a book for pleasure.
- The second group was asked how likely they were to floss their teeth within the following two weeks.
- The final group was asked to estimate how likely one of their classmates was to floss his or her teeth within the next two weeks.

Two weeks later, Levav and Fitzsimons asked all of the students to report how many times they had flossed their teeth in the preceding two weeks. Participants in the first group (who had been asked initially about their likelihood of reading a book) said they flossed 4.23 times in the preceding two weeks. But participants who had been asked how likely they were to floss actually ended up flossing 6.25 times.

The difference between flossing 6.25 times and 4.23 times may not seem much, but that works out as an uplift in flossing of nearly 50 per cent. Imagine being able to boost the incidence of anyone's behaviour by 50 per cent. That could be 50 per cent more customers buying your product or service. Fifty per cent more donors opening up their wallets to support the charity you're championing. Fifty per cent more of your friends and family doing what you think is best for them.

Just looking at those results, you could contend that the experiment only proves that asking a question about flossing simply reminds people to floss. But that's not the case.

I say that the investigation was ingenious because of the third group that Levav and Fitzsimons included in the study. The participants in the final group had been asked how likely one of their classmates was to floss his or her teeth. So they too had been reminded about flossing. But the participants in this group only ended up flossing 4.11 times. In other words, mentioning flossing to them by asking about the intentions of *other people* to floss led to no more flossing than asking them the completely unrelated question about reading for pleasure.[28]

It's an intriguing set of findings because it shows that questions are more than just hypothetical enquiries. Ask questions and you may influence real behaviour.

Asking questions with a purpose

Multiple studies demonstrate that asking people questions can guide how they behave. Get homeowners to estimate the chances of their buying a new car within the next six months and the idea may blossom as a desire to actually buy a new car. Ask employees to evaluate the likelihood of their using the new computer system at work and they may become intrigued enough to use it.

But even asking rhetorical questions – to which there's an implied right answer – may affect people's behaviour, too. Again, studies tell us that getting anybody to make even the flimsiest verbal commitment may subtly alter their behaviour. Consider the following examples:

- "Will you leave today and set up an appointment to get your children vaccinated against this disease?"

(Continued)

155

- "If you want to chart a path to personal success, will you visit my website and download a free information pack?"
- "I have pride in the service that we deliver to our customers. Will you join me in offering our customers the very best experience possible?"

The brilliant thing about questions is that you can ask them in almost whatever situation you're in. You can ask a single individual, say a young child, a question such as, "At lunchtime today, will you eat some salad with your meal instead of fries?" or "Will you do your homework this evening?" You can ask questions of a packed auditorium. You can even ask questions if you're being videoed for a clip you're going to post online or in a press release you're issuing by email.

So what questions would *you* ask?

Extending your repertoire of winning words

Standing out often requires communicating in a way that makes people feel, think or act differently. But if there's a running theme to this chapter, it's that information is not the same as influence. Education too often falls on deaf ears: simply telling people reasons why they should change their minds is rarely enough. That's as true for far-reaching goals such as boosting rates of organ donation or locking in votes for a politician as it is for pragmatic ones such as securing investment for your business or shifting more product.

Information is not the same as influence. In this chapter, we unpacked an evidence-based box full of tips and techniques for piercing people's indifference and helping our messages hit

156

home. But always begin by considering the needs of each specific audience. Which techniques may work best in each setting? At times you may wish to wield the hammer of emotion; at other times, metaphors and other imagery to chisel away opposition. Occasionally personal stories or perhaps something else entirely to smooth down any remaining resistance. Persuasion doesn't come from throwing everything at an audience but from choosing what you think will work best based on each audience's background, their wants, their hopes, their fears.

Extending your repertoire of verbal tactics

How do you improve your impact? Well, awareness of the different techniques is a good start. But then becoming more impactful is about incorporating the tactics into your speeches and presentations, your discussions and conversations.

Some thoughts:

- **Begin by observing people more closely.** Take note of the devices that they use. And when they use one that works well – a story at a party or a moral statement at work, for example – try to analyse why it worked.
- **Go into conversations and presentations with the intention of working on a specific tactic.** Don't just leave it to chance. Prepare a list or acronym for your next team meeting. Decide on an anecdote you can tell at Friday night drinks to impress your friends or make them smile. Practise and eventually the tactics will feel more comfortable, more natural.
- **Ask friends or colleagues to critique you.** Tell someone you trust that you want to get better at deploying contrasts and lists or anything else. Don't just rely on your own unreliable judgement about how good or bad you are. Get feedback on how you actually did.

In the first three chapters of this book, we have established that people can help themselves to stand out by presenting themselves and their arguments differently, by using psychological, nonverbal and verbal techniques, in effect to stage-manage their impact. So the old truism that "it's not what you say but how you say it" has a very strong basis in fact. But I'd hate to give the impression that standout individuals only succeed because they manage to manipulate audiences – that they succeed through the triumph of style over substance alone.

In our next chapter, we will discuss how standout individuals get noticed for their work achievements. After all, hard work and actually being good at your job must count, too. Right?

Well, sort of.

Onwards and upwards

- Remember, remember, remember that people are rarely – if ever – convinced solely by facts and logic. Human beings have both a head and a heart. Take the time to wrap the core of your message in deftly chosen language and you may find your message becomes that much more effective.
- Bear in mind that audiences are rarely the same. Of course it may be easier for you to reuse the same pitch, the same slides, the same message. However, consider that most audiences – whether that's one person or a roomful – want to be treated and spoken to as individuals.
- Given that people often follow heart more than head, reflect on the emotions you want an audience to feel. Dozens of studies have demonstrated the power of emotions in influencing behaviour. Start with an emotion in mind if you wish to be truly persuasive.
- Consider that techniques such as setting high expectations and using moral arguments also play to hearts rather than heads.

People may understand numbers, but they can be moved by superhuman ambitions and their morals.

- Tell more stories. That could be an inspirational story about someone who achieved success or a tale of failure to serve as a warning. Or share autobiographical anecdotes about your own life too. Everyone loves to hear stories. And wanting, actually wanting, to hear what you have to say is already half the battle.

- Consider also the tools most often used by professional orators: metaphors, analogies, similes, rhetorical questions, contrasts and lists. But remember that it's not just the presence of these that makes for a good impression. You need to sell them with nonverbal conviction too.

4

Augmenting Performance through Passion

There is no substitute for hard work.
Thomas Edison

What would you do with your life if you were a multimillionaire? Indulge me for a moment and imagine you have won the lottery and are in line to receive £10 million.

So that's a 10 followed by six zeroes: £10,000,000. That's a heckuva lot of money. And it's tax-free too. There would be no more mortgage to worry about. No bills to fret over ever again. Of course, if you're stupid and squander it on lavish holidays, fast cars and mansions, it won't last long at all. But if you're sensible, you could retire and live out your days enjoying a very comfortable life indeed.

So what would you do with your time?

Entrepreneur Julian Ranger found himself with the opportunity to do whatever he wanted to do with his life back in 2005 when he sold his business STASYS to the American aerospace and defence giant Lockheed Martin. The terms of the sale remain confidential, but when I asked him about his proceeds from the deal, he said: "I had the option not to work ever again. I had to work for two years as part of the deal. But after that I could easily have retired, bought a place in the south of France and done nothing."

I first met Ranger in 2009 and featured him in a previous book in a chapter on setting long-term goals and balancing work and life.[1] But when it became time for me to profile someone who seems to love their work, I could still think of no one better than him. And this in spite of the fact I have encountered many other entrepreneurs and business leaders in my work. He continues to stand out because of the joy he gets from working; unabashed enthusiasm radiates from him whenever he talks about his latest venture.

After selling his business to Lockheed Martin, he toyed with the idea of merely dabbling: of taking on a couple of nonexecutive positions, investing in up-and-coming businesses and perhaps working just a couple of days a month. But it wasn't long before he got the entrepreneurial itch again: he decided to thrust himself wholeheartedly into full-time work and the pursuit of building another successful business.

So why does he continue to work? Why push himself when he could be taking it easy?

"I still want to do something significant. Having built a business before, I have an idea and I want to pursue it. Not pursuing it would be more painful than pursuing it," said Ranger.

He actively revels in his work, although he stresses that he's not a workaholic. He has a loving family life, a thriving social life and sporting pursuits. However, empire-building remains an integral part of his identity.

"Work is an essential part of who I am. It keeps my brain interested and active. You can't take the work out of me as it's who I am. Trying to innovate is just what I enjoy," he added.

Do successful, standout individuals have fun because of their achievements?

The 51-year-old is quietly talkative, affable company. He has the build of an ex-rugby player but the quicksilver mind of an elite academic: whenever he answers a question, a torrent of words splashes out of his mouth as he flows from one topic to the next, the inner workings of his brain seemingly unable to dam the thoughts within.

His current enterprise is digi.me, an online business aimed at helping consumers keep track of, back up and protect all of their data. He believes that consumers are on the cusp of wanting more control over their data. So suppose a typical person has profiles on Facebook, Twitter and Whatsapp as well as perhaps shopping preferences on Amazon, music lists on Spotify and even banking data with HSBC or Barclays. What happens if one of those businesses gets hacked? Or loses the data? Or decides to sell it on to a third party?

Ranger is certain that digi.me – a name he chose to reflect people's online presence, their "digital me" – has the potential to become a billion-dollar business by 2020. And with his business pedigree, I would not bet against him.

However, it's not the promise of some tremendous future financial reward that drives him. Yes, some wannabe moguls throw themselves into their work in the hopes they will win big. But Ranger already won big. He made his millions. He can already afford to buy the yacht, the flashy cars, the beachfront properties all around the world. He could lie on a sun lounger for the rest of his life if he chose. But he chooses not to: he is savouring the business journey as much as the destination.

"I just love thinking. I like to come up with answers to problems. I enjoy engaging with people and persuading them that you've got a good solution; that's an enjoyable process. Demonstrating and trying to sell and get your ideas accepted, that's also interesting. It's fun," he said.

Every time I meet him, I find myself being infected by his enthusiasm. His face lights up, the edges of his eyes crinkling as he describes the magnitude of the challenges facing him.

Most people probably wouldn't be able to say when Ranger is working and when he is playing. In his world, the distinction between work and play isn't a clear one. One flows quite naturally and pretty pleasurably into the other.

Not that every day is fun. Being at the helm of a burgeoning business isn't easy. He has made mistakes, got the timing wrong on things, invested in ideas that didn't pay off. And running any enterprise is a perpetual juggling act of keeping employees, customers and investors happy – or at least trying to. But the good tends to outweigh the bad.

"If you didn't enjoy it, if the work wasn't an essential part of me, it would be difficult to get through the hard parts. There's no such thing as an unbroken stream of success. There will always be hard times. Unless you enjoy the whole thing, you're just not going to be able to cope with the downsides."

People like Ranger take sublime pleasure from their work *and* perform well. Indeed, the two often go hand-in-hand in many high achievers. But which is the cause and which the effect?

Do successful, standout individuals have fun because of their achievements? That being the case, success would be the cause and enjoyment a natural by-product. Or do people who enjoy their work – who find not only joy but also real meaning in it – end up accomplishing greater things? If this latter situation is true, it suggests that pleasure is momentously important if we wish to achieve any real measure of success.

Exploring the link between ardour and attainment

We could hypothesize and squabble about the links between passion and performance all day. But thankfully we can avoid going in circles by looking at a 2014 study published in the highly regarded *Journal of Experimental Social Psychology* by Duke University academic psychologists Paul O'Keefe and Lisa Linnenbrink-Garcia.

Let's pretend briefly that you've agreed to come into my laboratory to take part in a psychology experiment. I'm not there to run it but my chatty research assistant Becky explains that you will sit at a computer and be presented with five-letter anagrams to unscramble. Your task is to turn as many of these anagrams into real English words as you can. And you'll have just five minutes to do it.

For example, if you see the letters TOOPH flash up on screen, the right answer would be to come up with the word "photo".

But before you start, she asks if you would mind answering a few questions. How interested are you in completing anagrams? How exciting do you find completing anagrams?

She then mentions that a previous scientific trial has demonstrated that: "The anagrams you will be working on have been shown to be diagnostic of intellectual ability." Translating it into English: do well and that means you're a fairly bright person overall.

If you like, you can have a go at solving a few right now. The average person in O'Keefe and Linnenbrink-Garcia's study managed to solve 25 anagrams in five minutes. If you're up for a little challenge, you could set a timer and see how well you measure up. I'll put the answers into the numbered notes at the back of the book:[2]

BEYAB	TRESE	KEOJS	JANNI	GHILT
RATET	ZZIFY	TUORE	ILSSA	EDNES
ADDEJ	REZAG	RATSE	PEXEL	NAITS
IDSLA	TOLAL	RENAY	RETOW	GINOD
DERIC	LORCA	VREOL	SKEEN	YULCK
PUNTI	BREHS	FRIGE	PHEDT	KRASP
PUMST	VABER	XELAR	WHECY	WEBOL
KHALC	CMASK	NUCHH	WULAF	KLOFS

So imagine you've completed the test. Your five minutes is up.

Immediately, Becky comes back with a small steel and plastic handgrip – the kind people use to develop their grip strength. She asks you to squeeze it shut in your hand for as long as you can. She perches on the desk with a stopwatch to see how long you can keep your grasp tight.

After a few minutes, your hand starts to ache and eventually you have to admit defeat. And that's it. Experiment over. Thanks very much for your time!

What's going on? What were the experimenters trying to prove?

O'Keefe and Linnenbrink-Garcia were interested in two psychological concepts. The first was the extent to which participants said that they would enjoy solving anagrams. Most people weren't that bothered about completing anagrams; a few of the participants said they really didn't like solving anagrams and a handful of others said they absolutely loved them. Unsurprisingly, the scientific collaborators found that those who said they enjoyed tackling anagrams tended to solve more anagrams than those who enjoyed completing them less. That confirms what we already know: people who get a kick out of a task work more productively at it.

People who get a kick out of a task work more productively at it.

But there was a more exciting twist to come. I said that the research team was interested in measuring two psychological concepts and the second was to do with how much value participants derived from the task. Without telling their participants, O'Keefe and Linnenbrink-Garcia had split the participants into two groups and told them something different about the meaning of the anagram task:

- One group was told (as you were told): "The anagrams you will be working on have been shown to be diagnostic of intellectual ability."
- A second group was told: "The anagrams you will be working on have not been shown to be diagnostic of intellectual ability."

So the first group believed that solving anagrams was a measure of intelligence or like a form of brain training. The others thought it was just a frivolous task, a fruitless waste of time. Looking again at people's performance on the anagrams, the researchers found that the participants who did best were those who felt that it was *both* fun *and* valuable.[3]

Remember that everyone was granted the same five minutes for the task. So participants didn't perform better because they stuck with it longer; they did better because they were more efficient. In other words, enjoying what we're doing *and* feeling that it's valuable helps us to reach peak

Enjoying what we're doing *and* feeling that it's valuable helps us to reach peak levels of performance.

167

levels of performance. To use the vernacular, we can find ourselves firing on all cylinders.

This humble study throws up some significant implications. By altering people's perception of the value of the task, O'Keefe and Linnenbrink-Garcia demonstrated that value is something we conjure up in our heads rather than a given. And that may make a real difference to what we will be able to accomplish.

Choosing how we make sense of the world

The anagram experiment tells us that value is a mental construct. It's a *belief* that can be changed – that *we* can change. It's not an immutable property of the world. It's not like the height of a person or the weight of an object, which are fixed physical properties. Neither is it like the number of hours we're expected to be at work or the volume of emails we need to plough through every day, which may be out of our control.

As human beings, we can choose to believe that tasks, duties or projects are more or less valuable. We can imbue assignments and chores with more or less meaning. Simply believing that something has more intellectual worth and value may help us to perform better at it. And that must be a good thing indeed. After all, who doesn't want to be recognized as a standout, star performer?

Injecting meaning into your work

The idea of the value of your work may seem fluffy and inconsequential. But it's not. Remember that I'm not advocating that you attribute meaning to your work merely because it will make you feel better. No. The study by O'Keefe and Linnenbrink-Garcia tells us that attaching greater value to a task can stoke your efficiency. It's a seemingly soft route to hard results, to greater productivity and performance.

Studies have found that people can voluntarily attach different values and meanings to the same tasks. But it's not for me to dictate what values you should ascribe to your work. Have a go and decide for yourself using this exercise based on one used by Yale University professor of psychology Geoffrey Cohen and his colleagues.[4]

Below is a list of characteristics and values, some of which may be important to you, some of which may be unimportant. Please pick the five qualities and values that are of most importance to you.

Art/aesthetic appreciation	Sense of humour	Status
Control	Kindness	Health
Freedom	Fun	Creativity
Spontaneity/living in the moment	Spiritual growth	Relations with family
Love	Sporting achievement	Wealth
Helping others	Integrity	Relations with friends

When you've got your top 5, rank them in order of their importance to you from 1 to 5, where 1 represents the most important one and 5 the least important one. No ties are allowed!

Finally, spend six minutes writing about your number 1 value. Why is your value important to you? And describe a time in your life when it has been particularly important.

(Continued)

169

Need proof that it works? Psychologist Brandon Schmeichel at Texas A&M University and marketing researcher Kathleen Vohs at the University of Minnesota set out to test this precise values-based writing exercise. After extensive testing, the social scientists concluded: "Calling up one's guiding principles in life temporarily improves performance."[5]

So remind yourself of your values and see if you can find ways to link your values to your work. Rather than seeing your work merely as a set of tasks that need doing, think about the connection between your work and your personal goals and values. Does your work provide you with the platform to pursue your sporting achievements, relations with family or artistic leanings? Or maybe you can find ways to live your values at work – to do your work with integrity or by living in the moment, utilizing your creativity or being in control, for example.

Note that Schmeichel and Vohs found that values-based writing only *temporarily* boosts performance. That means that the exercise can't be a one-off intervention; it has to be revisited occasionally. And somewhat counterintuitively, reconsidering your values may be of most benefit when you're at your busiest.

Huh? Why ponder your values when you may have a hundred more pressing affairs?

When you're feeling swamped by reports, meetings, spreadsheets and enough work to make your heart sink, you naturally want to crack on with it all. But it's precisely when you're feeling inundated that you may benefit most from a jump in your efficiency. Taking just six minutes out of your day to review your values may be a savvy investment: reminding yourself why you do what you do may help you to recharge and enhance your efficiency for the tasks ahead.

170

If that values-based exercise seems like mental self-trickery, you would be at least partly right. But much of human life hinges on the psychological games that we play with ourselves. As we saw in Chapter 1, confidence is often a contest lost or won squarely on the battlefields of our own minds. People who feel anxious or depressed often have lives that are no objectively different from those who feel confident and capable –

Reflecting on our deepest values and how we live in tune with them has quantifiable benefits.

they may differ only in the messages that they tell themselves.

Success or defeat in many arenas – spanning sports, business and even relationships – can come down to our beliefs about ourselves and the world we live in. It's tempting to dismiss the importance of values because we can't see or touch them, buy or sell them. However, the experimental evidence tells us that they are very much consequential. Reflecting on our deepest values and how we live in tune with them has quantifiable benefits. So how might you alter the extent to which you believe your work has value?

Imbuing meaning into the work of others

If you manage people, there's more to learn from O'Keefe and Linnenbrink-Garcia's study. The ramification is that you can help your colleagues or employees to attach greater importance and value to *their* work too.

The more you can help them believe their work is meaningful and valuable, the better they will perform. Help others to focus on the mission, purpose or values underlying what they're doing. Even reminding people of the bigger picture and the ways that their work may assist others – whether that's customers, co-workers or anyone else – may boost the value and significance they attach to their work.

Linking passion to performance

We're still not done with the study by O'Keefe and Linnenbrink-Garcia, though. To recap, they concluded that people who found work enjoyable or meaningful tended to perform better – more efficiently – than those who didn't. But, hang on, what was the handgrip part of the proceedings about?

The investigators observed that participants who found the anagram task dull and meaningless gave up on squeezing the handgrip far more quickly than those who enjoyed or valued the anagrams. To put it another way, those who found the task boring or trivial became worn out sooner.

Clearly, sitting at a desk solving anagrams was not a *physically* demanding task. It's not like having to lift heavy weights. But doing the anagram task *mentally* exhausted those participants who felt the task was tedious or futile. These hapless souls had less willpower – what psychologists call "self-regulatory resources" – to spare.

However, those who found the anagram task enjoyable or valuable were able to clutch the handgrip for longer. They still had willpower to spare. After having done the anagram task, they still had the motivation to go on and perform well on the handgrip task too.

All of this talk about self-discipline and the motivation to go on may seem a little dry. So let's see how this could help us in practice. Suppose two friends, Helen and Christina, both work 10 hours a day as marketing executives for the same firm. They have the same boss and even sit at desks next to each other. Helen gets a big kick out of her job, while Christina merely tolerates it.

It's the start of the week. On arriving at the office on a Monday morning, they both check their email. Unsurprisingly, they already have dozens of emails to wade through.

Christina doesn't hate her work but she could definitely think of things she'd rather be doing. That lack of enjoyment and value means that she isn't exactly focused and efficient. So she takes 25 minutes to empty her inbox.

Enjoyment isn't just a nice-to-have – it's a must-have for performance in work and life.

On the other hand, Helen is quite entertained by reading her colleagues' and clients' thoughts and queries and – because her interest allows her to work more efficiently – takes maybe 20 minutes to sort through the same number of emails. So Helen is already up five minutes. Perhaps she can make herself a drink, catch up with a co-worker or spend a few minutes reflecting on her priorities for the day.

Moreover, O'Keefe and Linnenbrink-Garcia's study tells us that being slightly less engaged on the first task may also affect Christina's performance on her next task. Completing one unrewarding task drained some of her self-regulatory resources, her mental strength. Her next task will almost certainly not involve having to squeeze a handgrip, but whatever it is, she'll have less willpower for it.

So cheerless Christina's performance deteriorates little by little. Each time her self-regulatory resources and efficiency drop off, she will need to take longer to do the same task as one of her co-workers. The research suggests that – all other things being equal – she just can't work as productively as cheery Helen.

With less willpower to spare, Christina may find herself becoming more grouchy, too. When faced with even relatively innocuous requests from colleagues, she may find herself answering back rather more sharply than she would prefer.

To what extent do you love and value or feel drained by your work?

On the other hand, Helen has plentiful reserves of staying power. So she finds it easier to bite her lip, to be more tolerant and helpful.

Christina may continue to suffer even after work, too. Having had an emotionally draining day, she will have far less willpower at home. So she may more easily get annoyed by something her husband does. Or she may have so little strength of will left that she can only open a bottle of wine, drink more than is good for her and head to bed in exhaustion.

In contrast, because happy Helen enjoys her job, she has more willpower left. She has enough self-regulatory strength to behave jauntily with her husband. What's more, she may have so much self-discipline left that she resists that bottle of wine and decides to head to the gym instead.

The point of all of this? Engaging in activities we find interesting and valuable not only improves our performance. It also preserves our willpower so that we can pursue whatever other goals we have later in the day – whether they are to do with our work or not. Enjoyment isn't just a nice-to-have – it's a must-have for performance in work and life.

That's why certain individuals can work till 2 a.m. on a project but still turn up to work the next day feeling, well, if not exactly refreshed then at least ready for more. In the meantime, others may be able to work for only a limited stretch before having to take a break for coffee or to surf Facebook for a while.

If I think about my own work, I know in particular that writing books such as this one is something that I not only love but also value. Sometimes, I can be writing on a weekend and forget to eat. I'll look at a clock, see that it's 4 p.m. and realize that I've actually been really, really hungry for hours.

In contrast, I feel pretty drained when dealing with the financial side of my work – invoicing, working out cash flow, dealing with the accountant, sorting out tax matters and so on. If I do some financial stuff for even an hour, I often find myself craving a chocolate brownie or some other super-unhealthy sugary snack – probably because I've used up all of my so-called self-regulatory resources.

So what about you? To what extent do you love and value or feel drained by your work?

Diagnosing your true feelings about your work

Professor of organizational psychology Wilmar Schaufeli and a troop of researchers have developed a psychological test measuring work engagement – or the extent to which people feel switched on, engrossed and invigorated at work. It's a pretty robust test because it's based on a survey of over 14,000 respondents in 10 countries, including Germany, Norway, Spain and Canada.[6]

The idea is to read a number of statements about how you feel at work. You read each statement and decide how often you feel each statement describes you at work.

Here are a few examples of the kinds of statement in their questionnaire:

- At my work, I feel bursting with energy.
- I am enthusiastic about my job.
- My work inspires me.
- I feel happy when I am working intensely.
- I am proud of the work that I do.
- I get carried away when I am working.

Dozens of studies have found that people – office workers, teachers, nurses, flight attendants – who feel more engaged in

(*Continued*)

175

their jobs tend to perform better at them.[7] So the lesson is this: if you want to stand out by getting results and actually performing well, it really helps if you enjoy your work. You have to find your work sufficiently interesting and valuable that you feel engaged rather than drained by it.

So how do you feel when you read those statements? Are you thinking, "Yes, that's mostly me – I like my job!" or even, "Yes, that's definitely me – I love my work!"? Or do you look at the statements with a sense of dread, thinking that work is something you would most definitely want to quit if you could only afford it?

The reality is that most of us work because we need to put food on the table and keep a roof over our heads. Few of us have the financial resources to choose with total abandon how we spend our waking hours. But opening your eyes as to how you truly feel about your work may allow you to not only transform your relationship with your work but also turbocharge your performance. And who knows? Perform well enough and you may just get noticed for your achievements. That way, you may be able to put rather better food on the table or an even bigger roof over your head.

Moving from job design to job *crafting*

So how *do* you feel about your work? Of course there may be days when you feel either jaded or angry and wish you could be doing something else. There may also be amazing moments when everything comes together and you get the recognition you deserve. But don't look at the individual downs or ups. Think about the patterns and how you most habitually felt over the last 6 to 12 months, perhaps.

On a scale from 1 to 10, how engaged do you feel about your work? Perhaps you are scoring at the 8, 9, 10 end of the scale – where you feel bursting with energy, inspired and totally lose track of time when you're working. Maybe you are feeling at the 1, 2, 3 end of the scale and decidedly wearisome or maddened about **People who revel in their work are more likely to perform better.** everything to do with your work. Or maybe you're somewhere in the middle – neither massively despondent nor deliriously excited about work.

Remember that we're looking at enjoyment not because of touchy-feely notions about the meaning and purpose of life. This is about performance, results and getting noticed for the right reasons. The scientific evidence is clear: people who revel in their work are more likely to perform better. So look for ways to find gratification in your work not only for its own sake but because it will help you to be more successful too.

Excellent idea. How?

In an ideal world, your boss would help to shape your job so you could be optimally pro-ductive. Your boss would notice that you didn't like spreadsheets but that your colleague did – or vice versa – and would adjust both of your workloads accordingly. Perhaps you would like **Bosses don't have the time or energy to think about your needs.** more contact with customers while another col-league would like less. Again, your boss would have spotted this and would have designed both of your jobs accordingly. Or your boss would recognize that you were great at giving presentations and consequently give you further chances to shine even more.

Employers call these sorts of changes job *design*. It's about senior decision makers within an organization making alterations to how jobs, tasks and roles are structured. So your boss could either formally change your role or conditions or less formally just steer more of the right projects your way.

But let's get back to reality. You and I both know that we don't live in an ideal world. Bosses are invariably so busy trying to keep on top of their own workloads that they don't have the time or energy to think about your needs. Yes, they *should* be thinking about how best to design your job and those of your fellow workers. But things probably aren't going to turn out that way.

This regrettable truth about the modern-day workplace has led psychologists and other social scientists to look at ways in which individuals can modify their working environments for themselves. In 2001, researchers Amy Wrzesniewski then at New York University and Jane Dutton at the University of Michigan were probably the first to coin the phrase "job crafting" to describe the "the physical and cognitive changes individuals make in the task or relational boundaries of their work".[8]

Job crafting is about us as individuals taking responsibility and using our initiative.

Job crafting is about us as individuals taking responsibility and using our initiative to find ways to become more engaged and productive at work. Some of those changes may involve the tasks themselves – perhaps doing slightly less of the tasks you don't enjoy and slightly more of the ones you do. Or swapping tasks with a colleague, learning better ways to work, developing your own shortcuts and so on.

Other tweaks may have to do with the so-called relational boundaries or the people that we deal with and how we deal with them. For example, if you spend more time working with someone you get on with, that's clearly going to make work less tedious. Or if you can ask your boss or a colleague for more advice, that may make your job easier.

Job *design* is about waiting for people up above – head honchos and human resources departments – to change things for you. But job *crafting* is about taking responsibility and altering things for yourself. It's about depending on your own resourcefulness rather than waiting for someone to sort matters for you. Job crafting is about taking control and accepting that you can steer the direction of your career rather than waiting in the possibly vain hope that your bosses and colleagues will hand you what you seek.

Analysing your efforts at job crafting

Since the notion of job crafting was floated by Wrzesniewski and Dutton in 2001, it has received a lot of attention. Researchers and business school professors have implored people to craft their jobs in order to become more fulfilled – or at least less frustrated – and a lot has been written on the topic. And it's a lovely, compelling idea that we can all take charge and feel better about our working lives rather than merely wishing things were different. But studies haven't always been terribly helpful in telling us exactly *how* to do the whole job crafting thing.

Fast-forward just over a decade, though, and there's marvellous news. In 2012, Erasmus University Rotterdam academics Maria Tims, Arnold Bakker and Danntje Derks developed a job crafting questionnaire with specific implications on how to job craft. Before I describe it in too much detail, have a go at rating the extent to which you have tinkered and tweaked your job to suit you.

We can all take charge and feel better about our working lives.

Take a look at the 21 statements and rate the extent to which you feel that each statement describes your behaviours and attitudes at work. Be scathingly honest with yourself. No one else has to know

179

the answers and this is ultimately about helping you to feel more engaged and productive at work.

	1 – never	2 – seldom	3 – regularly	4 – often	5 – very often
1. I try to develop my capabilities.					
2. I try to develop myself professionally.					
3. I try to learn new things at work.					
4. I make sure that I use my capacities to the fullest.					
5. I decide on my own how I do things.					
6. I make sure that my work is mentally less intense.					
7. I try to ensure that my work is emotionally less intense.					
8. I manage my work so that I try to minimize contact with people whose problems affect me emotionally.					
9. I organize my work so as to minimize contact with people whose expectations are unrealistic.					

	1 – never	2 – seldom	3 – regularly	4 – often	5 – very often
10. I try to ensure that I do not have to make many difficult decisions at work.					
11. I organize my work in such a way as to make sure I do not have to concentrate for too long a period at once.					
12. I ask my supervisor to coach me.					
13. I ask whether my supervisor is satisfied with my work.					
14. I look to my supervisor for inspiration.					
15. I ask others for feedback on my job performance.					
16. I ask colleagues for advice.					
17. When an interesting project comes along, I offer myself proactively as project co-worker.					
18. If there are new developments, I am one of the first to learn about them and try them out.					

(Continued)

	1 – never	2 – seldom	3 – regularly	4 – often	5 – very often
19. When there is not much to do at work, I see it as a chance to start new projects.					
20. I regularly take on extra tasks even though I do not receive extra salary for them.					
21. I try to make my work more challenging by examining the underlying relationships between aspects of my job.					

Your score for the 21 statements give you scores for four different subskills of job crafting. Let's look at each in turn with a view to upgrading both your delight in your work and your performance.

1. Increasing structural job resources

Several studies have demonstrated that people who increase their structural job resources tend to be rated *by their colleagues* as both more employable and stronger performers at their jobs. Work out your *Increasing structural job resources* subskill score by adding up the scores you gave statements 1 to 5. So if you ticked "1 – never", that means you get one point; "4 – often" gets you four points and so on.

182

To do your job well, you need to have the right skills. So to what extent do you pursue training and learning opportunities?

In my second job working as a management consultant, my employer set aside a budget of up to £1,000 per consultant per year for going on training courses. But I'm sad to report that hardly anyone took up the opportunity to do so. My colleagues and I felt we were too busy servicing our clients to take two or three days out of the office to go on a training course.

Looking back, I realize now that we weren't too hectic at all. Maybe we arrogantly felt we simply didn't need further training. Or we felt that doing good client work would win us more kudos from our teammates than being lectured on some training course. In any case, it's one of my few regrets from having worked at that company that I didn't develop my capabilities and generally increase my structural job resources.

To what extent do you pursue training and learning opportunities?

Nowadays, there are so many different ways to develop ourselves. There are free MOOC (massively open online course) classes covering topics as varied as basic literacy, computer science, international human rights and quantum mechanics. Canvas Network, edX and Coursera are just some of the better-known providers of such courses.

Of course, we can go on actual training courses and workshops in which we sit and learn with other students in real time too. We can read books or watch online videos. We can ask colleagues for advice or shadow them and learn by observation.

It's not just our technical skills that we can work on either. For example, one client I'm working with is investing in his ability to manage stress. He meets with a therapist weekly and has integrated mindfulness meditation exercises into his life.

Neither is this subskill only about learning while away from the workplace. Statement 3 says, "I try to learn new things at work." That could be from asking to be put on projects that will develop your skills. That could be from talking to peers about their work. That could be from shadowing and observing others or anything else you can think of.

Perhaps the best summary of this job crafting subskill comes from statement 5, "I decide on my own how I do things." To me, this statement is about taking the initiative. Rather than waiting to be told how to do something, this is about finding a way to do a task that suits you. For example, I worked with a group of business development executives (salespeople by another name) at an accountancy firm. Some of the executives did most of their selling from their desks, by cold calling dozens of different firms every day. Others took a more personal approach and spent more time in face-to-face meetings. Neither approach was inherently better: one just suited some workers better than others.

2. Increasing social job resources

Maria Tims and her fellow creators of the questionnaire define "social job resources" as the availability of coaching from experts, and feedback and support from colleagues. So this subskill is about asking for help whenever you need it rather than feeling lost about anything at work. It's about asking workmates for candid feedback: "How well did I do that task exactly?" And then, if you didn't do it as well as you could have, asking, "What could I do differently next time for a better result?"

Colleagues are often more than happy to offer their feedback and suggestions. You often only have to ask.

And remember: the point of job crafting is that it's up to us as individuals to seek guidance and opportunities. So, sure, your boss may be a bit hopeless. And yes, technically it may be your line manager's job to give you regular feedback. For whatever reason – perhaps he or she is overwhelmed by the work, insufficiently skilled or just underinterested in managing people – you're not getting any useful feedback or guidance. But **It's up to us as individuals to seek guidance and opportunities.** the point is that job crafters take the initiative and manage to drag feedback out of people. If not your boss, then at least your colleagues.

For example, I once coached someone I'll call Janine Maguire, a product manager in a technology company. She commented bitterly that her manager treated her and her teammates like mushrooms: "He kept us in the dark." When I asked her about his vision of the department, she laughed and said that she had no idea whether he had a vision other than to run around like a headless chicken dealing with the endless crises that seemed to come his way.

Fed up with her circumstances, she got together with several of her colleagues to review things. They listed all of the problems they faced and came up with a set of recommendations for how the team could run more effectively; they decided to set an agenda for the product management group rather than merely reacting to the demands of the rest of the firm. They presented their ideas to their manager, who was surprisingly receptive.

Maguire also decided to book one-to-one meetings with her manager. She set up a recurring note in her calendar every two weeks to remind her to ask for an early-morning catch up. She scheduled in the meetings. She suggested the agenda. She put together a list of questions to ask her boss. And by actively managing him, she got the direction and guidance she desired.

Her final complaint: she was hungry for – but wasn't getting – more strategic insight about her work. So she decided to orchestrate occasional networking meetings with people outside of her company. She didn't want to spend too much more time working, so she could only manage one or two meetings a month. But it gave her a better sense of what was happening in the wider world outside of her particular company. It also gave her a more muscular sense of control – that she was in charge of her career and not dependent on the vagaries of her manager.

So how about you? To figure out the extent to which you engage in *Increasing social job resources*, add together your scores for statements 12 to 16.

3. Increasing challenging job demands

For this aspect of job crafting, calculate your *Increasing challenging job demands* score by adding up the scores you gave statements 17 to 21. Sure, you've probably got a lot on your plate. But engaged workers actually *increase* their job demands. Rather than shying away from work, they pursue *more* work that will challenge them.

Engaged workers actually *increase* their job demands. That may sound crazy. But remember that this isn't my personal opinion. It's research data telling us that people who chase *more* of the right kinds of projects may not only feel more happily engrossed in their work but perform better too. For example, a study published in 2012 found that workers who said they increased their challenging job demands were rated by their peers as being more productive.[9] So it's not just that individuals who take on more delude themselves that they perform better – they're actually judged to be more industrious by their co-workers.

For instance, I came across a software engineer I'll call Karol Baranowski. The remit of his job was firmly to do with developing new software, testing it and making sure that his modifications fit into the whole that his colleagues were working on. However, as the team continued to hire more software engineers, he voluntarily took on an informal role guiding new recruits. He wasn't paid to do it; he did it because he found it stimulating. He liked feeling he was helping out the younger generation – even though most of the recruits were only a few years younger than him in most instances.

As Baranowski became better known for mentoring newcomers, he mentioned it increasingly to his boss and has now formally accepted a different role within the business. He now devotes around a day a week having one-to-one discussions with new recruits, shepherding them and organizing external training for them. The fresh faces joining the firm get his insight and guidance. And he takes delight from seeing the team's work from their multiple perspectives. Everybody wins.

Or consider a friend of mine, a physiotherapist at a clinic employing a half-dozen physiotherapists and other health professionals. An avid tennis player, skier and all-round sports fan, she finds a peculiar joy in working with patients who have suffered sports injuries – and especially from tennis and skiing. So she shared this interest with her colleagues and encouraged them to pass such cases on to her. They don't pass *all* of their sports injury patients to her – they like to keep a balance in their own work too – but she gets at least some sports injury referrals from them. To the outside world, it may not appear that she has made much of a change but, subjectively speaking, she gets the biggest kick out of working with this group – so much so that she's considering a postgraduate research degree in which she would specialize in the efficacy of treatments for athletes.

4. Decreasing hindering job demands

And so we come to the fourth and final aspect of job crafting. You can calculate your *Decreasing hindering job demands* score by totalling your scores for statements 6 through 11.

However, unlike the other three subskills, *Decreasing hindering job demands* may actually have negative consequences. When Maria Tims and her partners initially devised and tested the job crafting questionnaire, they found that higher levels of *Decreasing hindering job demands* was actually related to greater cynicism about work. And a later study led by Utrecht University's Paraskevas Petrou found that people who reported reducing hindering job demands tended to experience lower levels of engagement.[10]

In other words, high scores on this subskill may be a bad thing. The more you try to evade the mental and emotional consequences of your work, the more disengaged, the more switched *off* you may become.

Minimizing contact with pesky individuals is like running away, a form of avoidance or even denial. Take a look back at the statements that make up this subskill and you will read about behaviours such as "I manage my work so that I try to minimize contact with people whose problems affect me emotionally" and "I organize my work so as to minimize contact with people whose expectations are unrealistic." If you think about it, minimizing contact with pesky individuals is like running away, a form of avoidance or even denial. It's effectively admitting defeat. It's not the kind of assertive, insistent behaviour of someone who is taking more control at work. It's quite the opposite: it's saying that you *can't* win.

Not long ago, I came across a salesperson I'll call Naomi Pederson. Her role was to build relationships with new clients. Once she had coaxed a new client to sign up, she passed the client relationship on to one of the account managers. Unfortunately, she was struggling to get on with a colleague I'll call Jose Mendoza.

Mendoza felt that his sales colleague was argumentative and abrasive. So he tried to minimize his contact with her. He communicated with her as little as possible and mainly by email, despite the fact that their desks were within 60 seconds' walk of each other.

This tactic may have helped him reduce the agitation he felt whenever he had to deal with Pederson. But it also meant that more issues slipped between the cracks. Miscommunication was more frequent and led to added problems with clients. By *Decreasing hindering job demands*, he wasn't tackling the issue. He was merely avoiding it. It was a path that would lead him to greater disengagement and cynicism rather than less.

Other statements to do with this aspect of job crafting include "I try to ensure that my work is emotionally less intense" and "I make sure that my work is mentally less intense." Sure, it's OK to take the occasional coffee break, go for a walk or check Facebook every now and then. But too much again is merely another form of evasion, of ignoring rather than tackling the issue.

Or consider the statement "I organize my work in such a way to make sure that I do not have to concentrate for too long a period at once." That's effectively saying that *I slack off* or *I don't want to work too hard*, isn't it?

Again, remember that it's not me saying that *Decreasing hindering job demands* is a bad thing. It is studies that have reached this conclusion. *Decreasing hindering job demands* is associated with lower engagement and performance at work. Trust what the research tells us.

Delving into your relationship with your work

If you like, you can capture the scores you gave the four subskills of job crafting here:

	Average score	Your score
Increasing structural job resources	21	
Increasing social job resources	16	
Increasing challenging job demands	17	
Decreasing hindering job demands	14	

So how do you measure up? On the first three subskills, a higher score implies that you are helping yourself to feel more engaged and to be more productive at work. But remember that *Decreasing hindering job demands* is *inversely* related to engagement. In other words, the higher your score – the more you avoid people and reduce the intensity of your work – the *less* engaged, the more out of control and overwhelmed you are likely to feel.

The job crafting questionnaire describes specific actions we can all take to feel more engaged.

The job crafting questionnaire describes specific actions we can all take to feel more engaged in our work. Even in work environments in which employees have detailed job descriptions and carefully delineated work procedures, certain individuals still manage to adapt their working situations. People find ways to develop their own skills, seek social support and guidance, give their work greater meaning, pursue more interesting work and face up to vexing individuals.

I have found the questionnaire a useful tool in my coaching and leadership development work because it points to actions that individuals can take to achieve both greater satisfaction and better performance. For instance, I recently used the questionnaire with a group of managers in the music and entertainment industry. The company was going through fairly seismic changes so the human resources department hired me to help the team reduce its stress levels and work together more effectively. Each manager completed the questionnaire and had a one-to-one discussion with me about its repercussions.

One manager I'll call Joanna Dunlop found her biggest weak spot was in *Decreasing hindering job demands*. A manager with a sharp sense of humour, she described the strong relationship she had with both her boss and her colleagues. However, she admitted that she struggled to ward off competing requests. She was both working long hours and feeling emotionally frazzled by attempting to juggle her teammates' many rival claims on her time. By trying to please everybody, she ended up getting involved in lots of projects but rarely delivering outstandingly.

However, after discussing matters in more detail, she decided that she needed to focus more on certain priority projects – the really big assignments and decisions that made the biggest difference to her work and the department's objectives. She needed to say no more often to the less weighty demands being made of her rather than trying to do everything.

Crafting the perfect career

Many of the most successful people have realized that no one is going to hand them the perfect career. Somewhere along the way, they have learnt that it's up to them to create for themselves the work and life they desire. One of the best examples I've encountered of someone who has deftly made the most of her career is human resources professional Kate Griffiths-Lambeth.

I first worked with Griffiths-Lambeth nearly a decade ago while she was Head of HR for a division of the then-banking giant Lloyds TSB. She is currently Global Head of HR at Stonehage, an advisory business with offices worldwide catering to the needs of extremely wealthy jet-setting individuals and their families. And in case you're wondering whether that applies to you, you need a *minimum* of $25 million in the bank to qualify.

Over the course of her 30-year career she has moved from one job to the next roughly every two to three years. But what I find most interesting is that she has frequently been sought out for jobs. Rather than having to hunt around and apply for jobs like everybody else, she has more often than not been in the enviable position of having head-hunters and employers trying to woo her. It's a rather enviable situation: to be offered jobs, to be able to pick and choose rather than having to chase jobs down. How has she managed to become so hotly pursued?

"I'm very bad at saying no to things but I know that I learn and grow through them," she said in a cut-glass accent. Each time we met, I thought that she bore a resemblance to Kathleen Turner, the notably glamorous American film and stage actress.

To gain insight into the ways she has made herself so indispensable, I asked her to complete the job crafting questionnaire that we encountered earlier in this chapter. But it was only when we discussed her questionnaire responses that it became apparent why she has been so successful.

For example, in response to statement 1 ("I try to develop my capabilities"), she ticked the box for "5 – very often". I asked her to explain.

"I've always liked learning. I've always liked developing my skills," she told me.

Last year, for instance, she put herself forward and was elected a public governor of Guy's and St Thomas' NHS Foundation Trust. Working with a council of governors made up of professors, patients and staff, she helps to hold the hospitals publicly accountable for the services they provide.

In the last few years, she has also taught herself how to use social media and carved a niche for herself online. She has been active on Twitter since 2009 and began a regular blog in 2011.

"I have always liked keeping abreast of developments and one of the quickest ways of doing that is through technology," she explained.

"I'm becoming increasingly involved with social media because I can see things that are happening in other sectors that I might not be directly involved in."

Strictly speaking, becoming a governor of a large hospital trust may seem unrelated to her work as a human resources director. Neither does learning about social media and tweeting have much direct relevance to her work. But for her, that's almost precisely the point.

"Frequently, it will be something out in a completely different arena that will give me fresh ideas."

A case in point: at her firm, Stonehage, the finance department was at one point very overstretched. However, in her work at the hospital trust, she came across a piece of software that she was immediately able to pass on to her colleagues in finance.

Many of the most successful people have realized that no one is going to hand them the perfect career.

"You wouldn't automatically go hunting around the National Health Service for a solution," she said. "But actually the problems aren't that different once you scrape the surface off. So it's about being open-minded enough to look for solutions in the not-so-obvious places, because they're still solutions."

Similarly, she often finds that her Twitter followers provide her with useful information and counsel. Recently, she was trying to hatch a more innovative way of rewarding employees within her business. For advice, she turned to Neil Morrison who heads up human resources at the publishing house Penguin Random House. How did she meet him? Not through a conference or networking event but online through Twitter.

Now it may not seem terribly remarkable that Griffiths-Lambeth has taken it upon herself to tweet and blog. But remember that she works in human resources, a profession more associated with people dealings than technology. And neither is she a young 20-something for whom social media has always been a reality. She's not even a 30- or 40-something.

I know of too many folks who dismiss out of hand new technologies, new ways of working, new pretty much *anything*. "I don't see the point of Facebook – I'd rather pick up the phone," the managing director of a luxury consumer goods company told me last year.

Sure, not everything that is new will be of use. But until you have tried it, how can you make a truly informed decision?

Without wishing to sound rude, Griffiths-Lambeth disproves the adage that old(er) dogs can't learn new tricks. And it's precisely these new tricks that keep her current and in demand.

Returning to the job crafting questionnaire, statement 10 says, "I try to ensure that I do not have to make many difficult decisions at work." Griffiths-Lambeth ticked that she "seldom" did so. Why? Wouldn't it be less mentally gruelling to take the easy road occasionally?

"I don't mind making difficult decisions at work," she said.

One thing that comes across is her strong will, her refreshing forthrightness. It's hard to doubt her when she issues such statements.

Consider a prior role when she was head of human resources at a law firm. The business had been growing successfully for a number of years but was hit especially hard by the banking crisis of 2007. As clients started defaulting on payments, the senior managers at the law firm recognized that the business was in trouble. They decided that a massive programme of redundancies was needed to save the firm. Of course, it fell to Griffiths-Lambeth's team to make the cuts.

She and her team were forced to axe 20 per cent of the workforce. Contemplate that for a moment: having to make one in every five employees redundant. Clearly, those who lost their jobs were anxious or incensed, or both. But even the survivors may have felt guilty and demoralized. Decisions don't come much more gruelling than having to lay off your colleagues, your peers, even your friends.

What could we – or should we – be doing to propel ourselves to greater things?

"The best you can do is to step forward and solve those problems in as good a way as you possibly can rather than stepping back from it because it feels difficult," added Griffiths-Lambeth.

"It's the kindest thing to do for everyone and I don't mean in a soft, mollycoddle kind of way. It almost comes down to common decency to treat people in the way you yourself would wish to be treated.

And if that means having a difficult conversation but being honest and straight and fair and trying to be supportive, that's what we do."

Remember that statement 10 ("I try to ensure that I do not have to make many difficult decisions at work") along with statements 6 to 9 all measure the job crafting scale of *Decreasing hindering job demands*. The research suggests that people who score more highly on this scale are *more* at risk of disengagement and burnout. So it's splendid news that Griffiths-Lambeth chooses to face the more harrowing decisions head-on.

To report on her scores to every statement on the job crafting questionnaire could easily fill a chapter. But I hope that Griffiths-Lambeth's recollections have been instructive. In my experience, the job crafting questionnaire affords us a handy series of prompts. It allows us to dig a little more profoundly into our relationships with our work. To what extent are we grabbing opportunities and facing up to the most fiendish aspects of our work? Are we seeking advice from colleagues and feedback on our flaws? What could we – or should we – be doing to propel ourselves to greater things?

Gaining insight from the job crafting questionnaire

Completing the job crafting questions probably took you a minute – maybe two at the most. But that's not where the real work lies. It's mulling over your responses to each statement that will really help you drive your career forwards. You'll feel more engaged with your work, perform better and hopefully stand out from your co-workers too.

Take a look back at every one of the 21 statements. Imagine having to describe to a colleague or friend why you scored yourself as you did. Hopefully, Griffiths-Lambeth's responses will give you an idea of how to do this.

Are you really as strong as you initially thought you were? Where are your weakest scores? And what steps could you take to craft your job further?

Leaving Griffiths-Lambeth, I was struck by a thought unrelated to the job crafting questionnaire. To me, she is an excellent example of someone who took a while to settle into a profession.

Sometimes, it can appear as if most successful people always knew where their passions lay and what they were destined to do. You may have heard entrepreneurs talking about how they sold lemonade as young kids or engineers or entertainers talking about how they saw in themselves their life's purpose aged 5. But I don't think such rarefied stories represent reality for the majority of people. The more mundane truth is that many – if not most – folks stumble around at least a handful of times before finding the right path.

Griffiths-Lambeth initially studied law at university with a career as a lawyer in mind. But upon graduating in the mid-1980s, she decided that the law wasn't for her and somehow became inspired to become a coffee trader for Cargill, a multinational agricultural services business. After a few years, she admitted that she then "tumbled" into a role as a derivatives dealer. A couple of years later, she saw an advert for a job as a recruitment consultant and swerved into yet another seemingly unrelated career.

Many folks stumble around at least a handful of times before finding the right path.

It took a few more years before she ended up in human resources, which is where she found her calling and thrived. So if you haven't discovered the perfect career for you yet, take heart.

197

For the first decade or more of Griffiths-Lambeth's working life, some observers may have derided her lack of a clear career path. They may have called her a dilettante or been reluctant to hire her because of her tendency to skip from one trade to the next. But, if anything, that kind of hopping from one discipline or industry to the next is an advantage in the increasingly fluid 21st century. The most innovative people are often able to bring ideas and expertise from other fields of work or sectors.

So don't try to settle too quickly into one profession. Feel free to traipse down different paths. Accept that 90-degree career turns can often give you unique experiences and skills. Think of each as an experiment, an opportunity to have a crack at something different and learn. And that's really the key: to keep learning at work, seeking advice and taking on as much as you can. And perhaps you too will have a career trajectory like that of Griffiths-Lambeth.

Putting job crafting into practice

Perhaps you're thinking that all of this talk of taking control and crafting a more suitable role sounds great in theory – but that it's aimed at people who are higher up the hierarchy than you. However, surveys tell us that's not the case.

A band of researchers headed by Justin Berg at the University of Michigan decided to measure the job crafting efforts of higher-ranked versus lower-ranked employees in both the for-profit and non-profit sectors. The higher-ranked directors and senior managers were responsible for tasks such as market analysis, strategizing, setting direction and managing teams of employees. The lower-ranked group comprised technicians and customer service representatives who did simpler tasks such as data entry, maintaining databases and responding to customer calls and emails.

Remarkably, though, the investigators found that both groups were able to engage in job crafting. True, they did it in different ways. But lower-ranked employees were just as able to take on new tasks and build relationships with people they wanted to work with as higher-ranked employees were.[11]

So don't assume that job crafting is only for *them* but not you. It's for all of us.

Crafting your work

Utrecht University scholar Machteld van den Heuvel and partners recommend that job crafting should be done over a month-long period. Rather than trying to change everything at once, they recommend tackling the four different aspects of job crafting one week at a time.[12]

Begin by getting hold of a new notebook or starting up a new document. At the start of each week, have a think about that particular job crafting subskill and work only on that one. During the week, keep detailed reports on your job crafting activities and reflect on your progress. What worked? What didn't work – or hasn't worked immediately? What else could you try?

If you're aching to boost not only your engagement but performance too, follow the four-week programme:

- **Week 1: Increase your social job resources.** Successful people turn to friends, colleagues and even faces outside the organization for guidance and support. That's kind of the definition of teamwork. So think collaboration and cooperation rather than having to soldier on alone. How could you get more feedback on your performance and build up the support you get from teammates, mentors, advisers and friends?

(Continued)

199

- **Week 2: Tackle your hindering job demands.** Remember that people who *Decrease hindering job demands* tend to be *less* engaged about their work and more cynical. So tackling hindering job demands isn't about running away and ignoring situations. Think about the most troubling, mentally exhausting parts of your work and consider how you could tackle these sources of stress. Could you have an honest conversation with that person with whom you always seem to be butting heads? Could you ask for assistance in making those tough decisions at work? But this is important so I'll say it again: be careful not to *reduce* your job performance by dodging tasks or people you really should be dealing with.
- **Week 3: Increase your challenging job demands.** Think about the kind of work that interests you most. Keep track of your mood and interest level. When you find stuff that makes you perk up, look for ways to do more of it. The more exciting, ambitious tasks you can do, the more invigorated you will feel and the more ready you will be to tackle the less thrilling tasks that need doing too.
- **Week 4: Increase your structural job resources.** What skills or topics would it help you to learn or develop further? This isn't just about working on your shortcomings – it may be more helpful at times to hone even further some of your existing strengths too. Statement 5 says "I decide on my own how I do things", so this is also about looking for ways to tackle tasks and projects in ways that suit you and get the best outcome – even if that sometimes isn't the "official" way of doing so.

If you really want to succeed in your attempt at job crafting, work over the course of a month with a buddy. Find someone – perhaps a colleague within your organization or just a friend anywhere else – with whom you can discuss each other's job crafting efforts. Perhaps talk through your ideas at the end of each week. Swap ideas and you may be able to help each other squeeze past further bottlenecks.

Studies on job crafting have been conducted in all sorts of industries, in both for-profit and non-profit organizations in Europe, North America and China.[13] And the proliferation of research all suggests the same thing: job crafting is a way for all of us to not only feel more engaged but also perform better.

As you develop new skills and get comfortable with them, you may need to invest in others.

It isn't a quick fix, though. The intervention suggested by van den Heuvel takes a month. But even that may be just the start of what should be an ongoing process. Clearly, as you develop new skills and get comfortable with them, you may need to invest in others. And just because you've expressed your interest in a particular type of work doesn't mean your colleagues will remember what you've said. You need to keep pursuing the matters that intrigue you. And as the world around you evolves, you need to keep adjusting what you do too.

Creating the i-deal job

Job crafting is about taking the initiative, seizing the steering wheel of our careers and shaping our work in often informal ways. But some people take things further.

Consider a friend I'll call Dominic Deering. He is a personal assistant and office manager for the London branch of a firm of accountants headquartered in Continental Europe. Having just celebrated his four-year anniversary at the firm, he decided he wanted to revise his working arrangements.

"My partner was working as a contractor and tended to have large chunks of time off so I wanted to be able to take more time off for us to travel together," the unassuming 39-year-old told me.

Also, Deering had once been a competitive ice figure skater in his teenage years capable of daring manoeuvres such as the triple Salchow; he had recently qualified as a figure skating judge, which sometimes required him to take mornings and occasionally whole days off at a time. The judging is unpaid but personally fulfilling. So he approached his boss and asked for more flexibility.

He got it. Rather than being paid a fixed salary, he negotiated a deal in which he gets paid on an hourly basis for the actual time he is at work.

Why would his employer allow him to work in such an idiosyncratic way?

"They like me and how I work. And because of the structuring of their London operation, it would be difficult for them to recruit a replacement, so my leverage was greater," he explained without arrogance.

"This saves them money and gives me the flexibility I require. It's the perfect situation. I am able to take time off for holidays and judging commitments or otherwise, as long as it's within reason."

If anything, he probably achieves more when he is in the office too. "I find that when I am at work I work more efficiently and effectively to complete what's required in the hours I'm able to do."

Employees who bargained over the nature of their jobs not only felt more positive *but also performed better.*

Such idiosyncratic deals have been dubbed "i-deals" by an international squad of researchers led by Severin Hornung at Hong Kong Polytechnic University. They define i-deals as "personalized changes in work and employment conditions that individual workers have successfully negotiated with their employer or its agents".[14]

202

So an i-deal could involve revisiting your responsibilities and what you do – doing more of certain desirable tasks or fewer less desirable tasks, for example. An i-deal could involve changing your working hours or agreeing to more flexible home-working arrangements. Or seeking your employer's support for your longer-term career aspirations through courses, mentoring, more challenging work, an MBA and so on.

Some employees haggle for such deals during the recruitment and interviewing process; they make it a condition of their employment before signing on the dotted line. But Hornung's team looked specifically at 187 professionals who negotiated i-deals long after they had been hired.

Cutting a long story short, the scientists found that i-deals were a true win–win situation. Employees who successfully negotiated i-deals reported that they found their work more gratifying. Psychological tests showed that they felt less stressed, more fired up, more exhilarated about their work.

Clearly, it's not a major revelation that getting their way made them happier. However, the researchers witnessed that these employees were also rated as being better workers by their supervisors. In other words, employees who bargained over the nature of their jobs not only felt more positive *but they also performed better*.

Why am I mentioning all of this? Well, let's explore what i-deals actually are.

Remember that the i-deals under scrutiny by Hornung and her associates were changes that *individual* workers negotiated. These weren't deals brokered by a union or some other collective body who took the lead. No, it was individuals who decided that they wanted something different or better from their work. They took the initiative themselves.

What's more, these deals were *successfully negotiated*. So it wasn't just individual employees wishing that their jobs were different or carping to workmates about their situations. They actually pursued what they wanted until they got real agreement from their employers.

Job crafting and i-deals are both about taking action, *doing* something. Our earlier discussion on job crafting essentially pinpointed that people who informally seek more control over the nature of their work tend to be happier and more effective. I think of i-deals as the next step, the formalized extension of job crafting. And yet again, we see that gaining more control leads to both greater enjoyment and higher performance.

Job crafting and i-deals are both about taking action, *doing* something. They are about customizing your work and career; about deciding what you want and making it happen rather than merely hoping, dreaming or praying that the rest of the world will see fit to give you what you desire.

That will involve a bit of thinking on your part to work out what you can reasonably request. Maybe observe role models who are happy and productive at work to figure out how they achieved it. Probably ask colleagues for counsel or discuss ideas with friends. Do some planning. Perhaps write up a proposal and ask your boss for a proper meeting in which to discuss options.

But none of that is inconceivable. Take Deering's case. He isn't a high-flying executive on a six-figure salary. He doesn't even work as a fee earner for the accountancy firm but in a relatively modest support role as a personal assistant and office manager. But because he had established himself as a hardworking employee, he was able to sort out a one-of-a-kind working arrangement that has seen his quality of life skyrocket.

Just as job crafting isn't something that can only be done by high-level executives with lots of power to shape their roles, negotiating a so-called i-deal isn't something that is reserved for high-ranking individuals. And doing so may make you not only happier but also a better performer.

If you really want to stand out at work, don't just read about what *other* people do. Do something about it for yourself.

Onwards and upwards

- Consider that high-performing, standout individuals tend to feel very positive about their work. That may sound obvious. But if that's the case, sticking in a job you hate probably means resigning yourself to the fact that you will never get noticed or promoted. If you don't like your job, do something about it.
- Remember that the value we attach to our work is subjective. Two people can do precisely the same work: one can feel stressed and demoralized; the other can feel upbeat and motivated. No one *has* to feel a certain way about work. We can all feel more motivated about our work if we *choose* to.
- If you manage other people or run a business, consider that one of your most important responsibilities may be ensuring that the individuals working for you value their work and find meaning in it. Help them to understand the bigger picture and consequences of their work for their colleagues, customers and community and you help them to perform at their best.
- One way to be happier at work would be to quit your job and find one that's better suited to you. However, bear in mind that the core doctrine of job crafting is that people can and do shape the nature of their existing jobs. Consider how you could tweak your tasks and responsibilities. Seek feedback and

advice from teammates and outright coaching from your manager. The more you feel in control, the more productive you may become.

- Ultimately, remember that standout individuals don't just talk a good game by using clever words and body language. They get results too. But it's hard to deliver if you don't genuinely take pleasure from your work. So invest in your own career by taking charge and creating the job you want to be doing.

Conclusions: Onwards, Upwards and Over to You

If you live long enough, you'll make mistakes. But if you learn from them you'll be a better person.

Bill Clinton

Working as an organizational psychologist isn't a desk job. I spend a lot of time with people: I coach managers, entrepreneurs and job hunters; I run workshops; I sit in on conversations between warring colleagues. Over the years, I've met and worked with many, many names and faces in industries including banking, technology, advertising, healthcare, airlines and fashion – to list just a few.

The truth is that too many of these meetings have faded entirely from memory. Why? Because not that many people truly stand out.

In contrast, truly standout people linger long in the mind. But often, it's not just that they are memorable. They are often different too: we *enjoy* spending time with them. We want to work with genuinely outstanding people, send opportunities their way or even simply hang out with them.

I was impressed by entrepreneur Richard Canterbury the first time I met him. Over successive meetings, that impression never wavered. The square-jawed 39-year-old speaks slowly – to the point of being laconic – yet with authority. He shares his thoughts honestly and unguardedly, in a way that inspires trust.

To tell you about the nature of his business, imagine walking into a branch of premium fast-food chain Pret A Manger and deciding to order one of their freshly made smoothies. On offer are choices such as the Berry Blast (raspberries, chopped mango, chia seeds and a squirt of acai juice) and the Coconut Crush (chopped mint, pineapple, lime and coconut water).

They sound rather yummy, right? Well, yes, they are scrumptious (but, no, I've not been paid a penny to endorse them).

Thing is, the smoothies are actually made by the Love Taste Co., the company that Canterbury founded in 2004. Since then, he has grown a multi-million-pound business providing frozen sachets of chopped fruit to cafés, fast-food outlets and businesses that want to provide their patrons and diners with freshly made smoothies. As well as Pret A Manger, his company lists Virgin Active gyms, the Champneys health spa chain and hundreds of restaurants and shops as customers.

He has a small sales team working for him. But he still spends a considerable chunk of his time pitching and selling to prospective customers.

"Over the summer, it's virtually every day. So from April through to August, I probably do three to five pitches a week," said Canterbury, running a hand through Superman-thick brown hair.

Clearly, a business that produces chilled smoothies will be busiest during the summer months when cafés and fast-food outlets want to offer people ice-cold drinks. It's September when we sit down to talk for the first time and it's clear from his body language that he's glad for a respite from the daily onslaught of having to win customers.

Winning the pitch for Pret A Manger was a particular triumph. Back in January 2011, Canterbury returned to the office after his Christmas break and wrote a target list of the five customers he coveted most. On his first day back in the office, he tracked down an email address for the managing director of Pret A Manger and fired off an email asking for just 10 minutes to demonstrate how his smoothies were better than what Pret A Manger was serving up at the time.

"To my surprise, he wrote back a few days later and he said, 'You've got 10 minutes,'" he recalled.

The eventual meeting ran to 20 minutes – still not long given how most meetings drag on and on. But by the end of it, he had secured a deal with his dream customer. And after a successful trial run in a handful of branches, his products are now on sale in hundreds of stores.

Clearly, Canterbury is a smooth, charismatic salesperson. Or at least he is now.

Because his journey has been littered with sales meetings that went badly, mistakes that he made, times when he felt unsettled and far from his best. He recalls a particularly bad meeting several years ago when he was invited to pitch his products to a large and potentially crucial customer. Unfortunately, he turned up late. He

We want to work with genuinely outstanding people, send opportunities their way or even simply hang out with them.

started by saying that the traffic was bad but then changed his mind and came clean.

"To be perfectly honest, I left too late," he admitted. "I turned up late and apologized. I'd been in the car for about three and a half hours and I needed to use the toilet."

When he was directed to the toilets, he found that they were occupied. Only the disabled toilet was available so he slipped in there. However, instead of pulling the cord to flush the toilet, he pulled the disabled alarm.

"The person I was meeting was stood there waiting for me and the alarm was ringing," he added.

Not the most auspicious start. If it's true that first impressions count, well, he had already turned up late *and* used the disabled toilet when he is fully able-bodied *and* caused a ruckus by accidentally setting off the alarm.

"I was under prepared. I felt flustered. Nothing went right in the meeting and I couldn't pull it back from there," he said.

But he learnt the lesson. Not just to be on time, but to turn up early enough so that he can put himself into the right frame of mind to make a great impression. He now frequently arrives at sales meetings up to an hour ahead of schedule.

"So for me it's really important to be prepared and have time. I have 10 minutes just before I go into the meeting to have a recap and a think about who I'm pitching to, what's important to them, what are the things I need to bring up that are going to clinch this sale," he said.

"In these 10 minutes of calm thinking, I write down in my book what the key messages are, the key points that I want to get across for this customer. I try to be very specific about the customer I'm seeing. So I'll just write five or six of those points down. Those might change during the meeting but I can go through them and come out of there and know I've covered all of the important points for that particular customer."

He has learnt the importance of allowing himself enough time for some mental rehearsal. So now he can prepare to engage fully with each specific customer every time.

Making the time to learn

Neither was the above incident the only time Canterbury has ever made a mistake. In our conversations, he recounted plenty of other gaffes and stumbles.

A more strategic example: his whole business was actually quite slow in taking off. Initially, he launched his business with the aim of opening smoothie bars – like coffee shops only serving fresh smoothies. Unfortunately, the process of negotiating property contracts, planning and building out each site took months and months. Eventually he realized that the glacial rate at which he was opening smoothie bars was not a lucrative proposition. But it took him a handful of years to figure that out. Some might say it was lost time; I see it as an integral part of his learning and figuring out how to make the smoothie business work.

I mention all of this not to embarrass Canterbury but to illustrate that even the most polished individuals weren't always that way. Often, the individuals who most draw our attention and become the targets of our envy can make affairs seem effortless. Standout salespeople, standout leaders, standout conference

Even the most polished individuals weren't always that way.

speakers, standout fundraisers and standout individuals from all walks of life – they can give off the impression that they are simply gifted, blessed, different. But what we don't see is all of the hard work that went into creating such effects.

The English saying about ducks is so true: while we may admire their serene progress across the surface of a pond, we can't see the frantic paddling that goes on beneath the water in order to propel them forwards. And the same is true for the noteworthy individuals we may encounter. We may remark upon their composure, their grace, their apparently easy talents. But we can't see the frequently tremendous efforts that have gone into making them appear that way.

Remember also the individuals we encountered in Chapter 1 (on confidence). People like Claire Mason, the public speaker who couldn't sleep or eat before gigs. Ralph Dixon, the seemingly cocky company director who was privately beset by the same worries that trouble us all. And highflier Julia Kryger, whom her colleagues described as a bountifully self-assured "power woman". To the outside world, they all seemed to be enviably talented and effortlessly successful. But in truth there was a lot of work that went into creating such appearances.

Those who make excuses or blame others are doomed to commit the same errors time and again.

The same is true of Richard Canterbury: he is a polished, charming individual. To my mind, there's no doubt that he is a standout sales person. But I was allowed a glimpse below the surface. To see all the hard work that went into turning him into the person that he is now.

In keeping with his flair for pitching, his company has been growing at a prodigious pace. Last year, the business ballooned by 74 per cent. In the current year – even though the end of the year is still some months away – the business grew another 68 per cent. To boost growth, the company has begun its international expansion plans and launched new products, including a range of vegetable smoothies. As we came to the conclusion of our conversations, I asked Canterbury whether he had any final thoughts to share from his career journey.

"I feel I'm halfway through it. I've got a long way to go," he replied.

And to me, that's a lovely thought. Despite his success, the flourishing growth of his business and his manifest talents, he still feels that he is a work in progress. The fact that he talked about his missteps with such candidness is a sign that he's willing to learn from them. Those who make excuses or blame others are doomed to commit the same errors time and again. But not him. No matter how good or even great he may be already, he's still itching to learn and grow.

Learning as you go

Any journey of self-improvement involves trial and error. Say you're trying to introduce more metaphors into your language. Some may work well while others fall flat. When trying to job craft, you may find that some of your efforts pay off handsomely while others end only in frustration.

Errors, mistakes and blunders are all perfectly fine – so long as you learn from them. In this book, we looked at how scientific researchers examined the effects of various interventions on groups of experimental subjects. I now invite you to think of yourself as a researcher looking at how our assortment of techniques works for you.

(Continued)

213

When something goes badly, learn from it. Reflect on what happened and analyse how you might improve on a future occasion.

But be systematic in reviewing your successes, too. Don't just try a technique and automatically assume that it worked as it should have done. Think back on how it went to suss out how it could go *even* better next time.

Whether I'm coaching an individual on a one-to-one basis or working with a group of managers, I recommend to most of my clients that they review their actions on a weekly or even *daily* basis. I suggest a simple method that I call **Plan, Do, Review**. The three steps are to:

- **Plan.** Identify what you want to do differently. Suppose you look back at the other chapters in this book and decide you wish to work on your nonverbal communication, your use of moral arguments or your confidence through the power paragraphs technique. Whatever you choose to do, think through how you will incorporate the new technique into what else you normally do. Perhaps write some notes on what you will do or say. Or mentally rehearse your words and actions.
- **Do.** The next step is to do it. You will only get better by trying new techniques, ideas and behaviours. So commit to a time and date to give it a shot.
- **Review.** Find the time soon after to reflect on how things went. If they went well, think about why they really worked and what you could do even better next time. If they didn't work out as well as you might have wished, consider what you could do differently instead.

Written down, the Plan, Do, Review system sounds almost patronizingly straightforward. But the benefit comes from doing it – not merely understanding it. Make plans, take action and then mull over the results – that's the way to a continuing cycle of personal improvement. Oh, and if you wanted more detail about its application, you might like to look at my last book *How to Win: The Argument, the Pitch, the Job, the Race* (also published by Capstone).

Smoothie entrepreneur Canterbury is someone who reviews his triumphs as well as his flops. One instance that he recalled was turning up to pitch his smoothies to employees at the headquarters of a major banking corporation.

Most of the time, he pitches to two or three people – a half-dozen at most. But on this occasion, he was faced with a crowd of 25. He didn't have enough smoothie mix to go around. And, because he only had one blender, the process was achingly slow. To top matters off, it was 4 o'clock on a Friday afternoon and everyone was watching the clock and itching to leave. Unsurprisingly, the meeting soured.

"They all just got up and left. I was left in the room feeling massively dejected and thinking I never want to let that happen again," remembered Canterbury.

"So now, even if I have to throw product away rather than use it, I'm totally, 100 per cent prepared."

People rarely get hit by great bolts of inspiration to become instant sensations.

Immediately after that disastrous meeting, he produced a checklist of everything he needed to take with him in order to pre-empt future surprises. Including enough product to whip up smoothies for up to 30 people.

"That was six years ago but every time, even now, I check every single box [on the checklist] to ensure that my bag has got everything in it including a backup blender."

He learnt from the experience. He reviewed what transpired and planned for it never to happen again by carrying around substantially more samples with him and creating an idiot-proof checklist.

No one would claim that Canterbury's lessons are earth-shattering revelations. These are not sensational insights that could set the world on fire. These are small alterations that helped him do business better little by little.

A little tweak here, a minor discovery there. But add it all up and look at him now.

Standing out is a skill honed over time. And that's how you could blossom too. Much as we might wish it otherwise, the truth is that people rarely get hit by great bolts of inspiration to become instant sensations. Becoming a standout individual isn't going to happen overnight. Indeed, expect too much, too quickly and you'll feel a failure. But *make time* to learn from the experiences you have each day and you will inevitably get better and better.

Standing out is a skill honed *over time*. Months will pass and one season may give way to the next. But I can tell you this: one day you will look back and suddenly realize that you're a whole lot better than you used to be.

Three final thoughts

Whether I'm presenting at a conference event to 1000 people or running a boot camp for a half-dozen leaders, I invariably conclude with a PowerPoint slide titled "Final thoughts". So I shall leave you with three closing observations.

Final thoughts

- Consider that success is like the tip of an iceberg – you don't usually see the hard work that went into other people's accomplishments

- Remember that insight (understanding) doesn't get results; it's implementation (actually doing things) that does

- Let me know how you get on – Twitter @robyeung or www.facebook.com/drrobyeung

© www.talentspace.co.uk

First, remember that what you see of other people rarely represents the whole truth. Someone may seem effortlessly confident. But beneath the surface they may be roiling with doubt. Someone else may appear to be an effortless presenter or public speaker. But you can't see the hours they may have spent writing their script, honing their language and rehearsing out loud; you can't know how many times they have worked at it over the months and years.

Keep that iceberg metaphor in mind. With effort and persistence on your part, you too can work on the chunks of the iceberg sunk below the surface and turn yourself into a more charismatic, influential, charming and standout individual.

A second but perhaps even more crucial thought: consider the immense difference between insight and implementation. If you finish this book and set it aside, you will gain very little. I say again and again to clients that insight – mere intellectual comprehension – is not enough. It's just like understanding the notion that physical exercise leads to weight loss. Understanding the theory isn't enough: you actually have to huff and puff to shed the pounds.

The same is true here. Sure, you may understand the principles of communicating more effectively using nonverbal cues and speaking techniques. You appreciate the theory behind becoming more confident and so on. But it's the application that matters. So make that plan. Try things out. See what techniques work for you. Insight does not lead to improvement; it's implementation that does.

Insight does not lead to improvement; it's implementation that does.

Lastly, get in touch. Do let me know what you think of this book. I too want to learn and grow as an author. I've written over 20 books and think that each book has got better. But I want my next one to be better still. Feel free to share your thoughts by writing a short review online – on a website such as goodreads.com or Amazon, for example. And then message me with the link to your review, OK?

Twitter: @robyeung

Facebook: www.facebook.com/drrobyeung

Onwards and upwards

- Adopt the mind-set of a scientist in analysing what works for you. Plan, do, review. Make a plan to test-drive a couple of techniques. Do what's in your plan. And then review what worked well or could work better next time.
- Consider your journey of self-improvement as a continuing series of experiments to discover what will help *you* be more eloquent and persuasive. Just because something works well for someone else doesn't mean it will be equally effective for

you. So don't assume you should follow anyone else's path. Put into practice the principles and techniques that work best for *you*.

- Accept also that any journey will involve stumbles and the occasional dead-end. Even the greatest entrepreneurs, scientists, leaders and geniuses of all time made mistakes. So it's probably safer to assume you will blunder and go wrong occasionally than to assume you will have an entirely smooth journey. But with the passage of time, you will eventually be able to look back and think, "Yes, I'm a lot better now than I was then!" With effort on your part, your progress is inevitable.

- Finally, remember, remember, remember: insight does not lead to improvement. Implement the techniques within this book if you really want to create a standout life and career. Go on. Have a go.

Notes

1. Boosting Self-belief and Debunking the Confidence Con

1 Or go directly to the link: http://www.youtube.com/watch?v=qemWRToNYJY, accessed 5th May 2015.

2 Adele opens up about her inspirations, looks and stage fright (April 28th 2011). *Rolling Stone*, http://www.rollingstone.com/music/news/adele-opens-up-about-her-inspirations-looks-and-stage-fright-20120210, accessed 5th May 2015.

3 Jordan, A. H., Monin, B., Dweck, C. S. *et al.* (2011). Misery has more company than people think: Underestimating the prevalence of others' negative emotions. *Personality and Social Psychology Bulletin*, 37, 120–35.

4 Brooks, A. W. (2013). Get excited: Reappraising pre-performance anxiety as excitement. *Journal of Experimental Psychology: General*, 143, 1144–58.

5 Savitsky, K. & Gilovich, T. (2003). The illusion of transparency and the alleviation of speech anxiety. *Journal of Experimental Social Psychology*, 61, 618–25.

6 Lammers, J., Dubois, D., Rucker, D. D. & Galinsky, A. D. (2013). Power gets the job: Priming power improves interview outcomes. *Journal of Experimental Social Psychology*, 49, 776–9.

7 Smith, P. K., Jostmann, N. B., Galinsky, A. D. & van Dijk, W. W. (2008). Lacking power impairs executive functions. *Psychological Science*, 19, 441–7.

8 Guinote, A. (2007). Power affects basic cognition: Increased attentional inhibition and flexibility. *Journal of Experimental Social Psychology*, 43, 685–97.

2. Persuading through Body Language and Nonverbal Communication

1   Friedman, H. S., Prince, L. M., Riggio, R. E. & DiMatteo, M. R. (1980). Understanding and assessing nonverbal expressiveness: The Affective Communication Test. *Journal of Personality and Social Psychology*, 39, 333–51.

2   Friedman, H. S., Riggio, R. E. & Casella, D. F. (1988). Nonverbal skill, personal charisma, and initial attraction. *Social Psychology Bulletin*, 14, 203–11.

3   Sabatelli, R. M. & Rubin, M. (1986). Nonverbal expressiveness and physical attractiveness as mediators of interpersonal perceptions. *Journal of Nonverbal Behavior*, 10, 120–33.

4   Shah, D. V., Hanna, A., Bucy, E. *et al.* (2015). The power of television images in a social media age: Linking biobehavioral and computational approaches via the second screen. *The Annals of the American Academy of Political and Social Science*, 659, 225–45.

5   Study shows expression just as important as words in presidential debates (13th January 2015). *Texas Tech Today*, http://today.ttu.edu/posts/2015/01/study-shows-expression-just-as-important-as-words-in-presidential-debates, accessed 5th May 2015.

6   André, E., Bevacqua, E., Heylen, D. *et al.* (2011). Non-verbal persuasion and communication in an affective agent. In: P. Petta, C. Pelachaud & R. Cowie (eds.), *Emotion-oriented Systems* (pp. 585–608). Berlin: Springer.

7   Puts, D. A., Apicella, C. L. & Cárdenas, R. A. (2012). Masculine voices signal men's threat potential in forager and industrial societies. *Proceedings of the Royal Society B*, 279, 601–9.

8   Feinberg, D. R., Jones, B. C., Little, A. C. *et al.* (2005). Manipulations of fundamental and formant frequencies influence the attractiveness of human male voices. *Animal Behaviour*, 69, 561–8.

9   Feinberg, D. R., Jones, B. C., DeBruine, L. M. *et al.* (2005). The voice and face of woman: One ornament that signals quality? *Evolution & Human Behavior*, 26, 398–408.

10 Miller, N., Maruyama, G., Beaber, R. J. & Valone, K. (1976). Speed of speech and persuasion. *Journal of Personality and Social Psychology*, 34, 615–24.

11 Apple, W., Streeter, L. A. & Krauss, R. M. (1979). Effects of pitch and speech rate on personal attributions. *Journal of Personality and Social Psychology*, 37, 715–27.

12 Leigh, T. W. & Summers, J. O. (2002). An initial evaluation of industrial buyers' impressions of salespersons' nonverbal cues. *Journal of Personal Selling & Sales Management*, 22, 41–53.

13 Maricchiolo, F., Gnisci, A., Bonaiuto, M. & Ficca, G. (2009). Effects of different types of hand gestures in persuasive speech on receivers' evaluations. *Language and Cognitive Processes*, 24, 239–66.

14 Maricchiolo, F., Livi, S., Bonaiuto, M. & Gnisci, A. (2011). Hands gestures and perceived influence in small group interaction. *Spanish Journal of Psychology*, 14, 755–64.

15 Clark, T. & Greatbatch, D. (2011). Audience perceptions of charismatic and non-charismatic oratory: The case of management gurus. *Leadership Quarterly*, 22, 22–32.

16 The idea of eager versus vigilant nonverbal styles comes from the work of Joseph Cesario and Edward Higgins. See: Cesario, J. & Higgins, E. T. (2008). Making message recipients "feel right": How nonverbal cues can increase persuasion. *Psychological Science*, 19, 415–20.

17 For an example of how matching nonverbal styles can boost the effectiveness of a message, see: Fennis, B. M. & Stel, M. (2011). The pantomime of persuasion: Fit between nonverbal communication and influence strategies. *Journal of Experimental Social Psychology*, 47, 806–10.

18 For a discussion of source confusion, see: Cesario, J., Grant, H. & Higgins, E. T. (2004). Regulatory fit and persuasion: Transfer from "feeling right". *Journal of Personality and Social Psychology*, 86, 388–404.

19 Lee, A. Y. & Aaker, J. L. (2004). Bringing the frame into focus: The influence of regulatory fit on processing fluency and persuasion. *Journal of Personality and Social Psychology*, 86, 205–18.

20 For an excellent summary of the differences between the eager versus vigilant styles, see: Cesario, J., Higgins, E. T. & Scholer, A. A. (2008). Regulatory fit and persuasion: Basic principles and remaining questions. *Social and Personality Psychology Compass*, 2, 444–63.

3. Winning with Words

1   Mayer, N. D. & Tormala, Z. L. (2010). "Think" versus "feel" framing effects in persuasion. *Personality and Social Psychology Bulletin*, 36, 443–54.

2   For a review, see: Brody, L. R. & Hall, J. A. (2000). Gender, emotion, and expression. In: M. Lewis & J. M. Haviland-Jones (eds.), *Handbook of Emotions: Part IV. Social/personality Issues* (pp. 325–414). New York: Guilford.

3   Hall, J. A. & Schmid Mast, M. (2008). Are women always more interpersonally sensitive than men? Impact of goals and content domain. *Personality and Social Psychology Bulletin*, 34, 144–55.

4   Han, S.-P. & Shavitt, S. (1994). Persuasion and culture: Advertising appeals in individualistic and collectivistic societies. *Journal of Experimental and Social Psychology*, 30, 326–50.

5   Uskul, A. K. & Oyserman, D. (2010). When message-frame fits salient cultural-frame, messages feel more persuasive. *Psychology & Health*, 25, 321–37.

6   General election turnout 1945–2010, UK Political Info, http://www.ukpolitical.info/Turnout45.htm, accessed 5th May 2015.

7   Panagopoulos, C. (2010). Affect, social pressure and prosocial motivation: Field experimental evidence of the mobilizing effects of pride, shame and publicizing voting behavior. *Political Behavior*, 32, 369–86.

8   Who is Microsoft's new business division leader Stephen Elop? http://www.computerworld.com/article/2538617/it-management/who-is-microsoft-s-new-business-division-leader--stephen-elop-.html, accessed 5th May 2015.

9   Nokia CEO Stephen Elop rallies troops in brutally honest "burning platform" memo? (update: it's real!), Retrieved January, 18 2015 from http://www.engadget.com/2011/02/08/nokia-ceo-stephen-elop-rallies-troops-in-brutally-honest-burnin, accessed 5th May 2015.

10 Witte, K. (1992). Putting the fear back into fear appeals: The Extended Parallel Process Model. *Communication Monographs*, 59, 329–49.

11 Witte, K. & Allen, M. (2000). A meta-analysis of fear appeals: Implications for effective public health campaigns. *Health Education & Behavior*, 27, 591–615.

12   Antonakis, J., Fenley, M. & Liechti, S. (2011). Can charisma be taught? Tests of two interventions. *Academy of Management Learning & Education*, 10, 374–96.

13   Amazon.com (2013). Overview, http://phx.corporate-ir.net/phoenix. zhtml?c=176060&p=irol-mediaKit, accessed 5th May 2015.

14   Locke, E. A. & Latham, G. P. (2002). Building a practically useful theory of goal setting and task motivation. *American Psychologist*, 57, 705–17.

15   Srivastava, A., Bartol, K. M. & Locke, E. A. (2006). Empowering leadership in management teams: Effects on knowledge sharing, efficacy, and performance. *Academy of Management Journal*, 49, 1239–51.

16   Bandura, A. (1977). Self-efficacy: Toward a unifying theory of behavioural change. *Psychological Review*, 84, 191–215.

17   Towler, A. J. (2003). Effects of charismatic influence training on attitudes, behavior, and performance. *Personnel Psychology*, 56, 363–81.

18   Emrich, C. G., Brower, H. H., Feldman, J. M. & Garland, H. (2001). Images in words: Presidential rhetoric, charisma, and greatness. *Administrative Science Quarterly*, 46, 527–57.

19   You can watch it on YouTube at: http://youtu.be/agKFUAf74bA.

20   Citron, F. M. M. & Goldberg, A. E. (2014). Metaphorical sentences are more emotionally engaging than their literal counterparts. *Journal of Cognitive Neuroscience*, 26, 2585–95.

21   Sopory, P. & Dillard, J. P. (2006). The persuasive effects of metaphor: A meta-analysis. *Human Communication Research*, 28, 382–419.

22   Shamir, B., House, R. J. & Arthur, M. B. (1993). The motivational effects of charismatic leadership: A self-concept based theory. *Organization Science*, 4, 577–94.

23   Haidt, J. (2007). The new synthesis in moral psychology. *Science*, 316, 998–1002.

24   For an example of a study showing that stories tend to influence people's behaviour more than facts when it comes to people's health, see: de Wit, J. B. F., Das, E. & Vet, R. (2008). What works best: Objective statistics or a personal testimonial? An assessment of the persuasive effects of different types of message evidence on risk perception. *Health Psychology*, 27, 110–15.

25 Herzenstein, M., Sonenshein, S. & Dholakia, U. M. (2011). Tell me a good story and I may lend you money: The role of narratives in peer-to-peer lending decisions. *Journal of Marketing Research*, 48, S138–49.

26 Den Hartog, D. N. & Verburg, R. M. (1997). Charisma and rhetoric: Communicative techniques of international business leaders. *Leadership Quarterly*, 8, 355–91.

27 Heritage, J. & Greatbatch, D. (1986). Generating applause: A study of rhetoric and response at party political conferences. *American Journal of Sociology*, 92, 110–57.

28 Levav, J. & Fitzsimons, G. J. (2006). When questions change behavior: The role of ease of representation. *Psychological Science*, 17, 207–13.

4. Augmenting Performance through Passion

1 The book was *E is for Exceptional: The New Science of Success*. Or, to give it its more formal reference: Yeung, R (2012), *E is for Exceptional: The New Science of Success*, London: Pan Books.

2 ABBEY STEER JOKES NINJA LIGHT. TREAT FIZZY ROUTE SAILS DENSE. JADED GRAZE STARE EXPEL SAINT. DIALS ATOLL YEARN WROTE DOING. CRIED CORAL LOVER KNEES LUCKY. INPUT HERBS GRIEF DEPTH SPARK. STUMP BRAVE RELAX CHEWY BOWEL. CHALK SMACK HUNCH AWFUL FOLKS.

3 O'Keefe, P. A. & Linnenbrink-Garcia, L. (2014). The role of interest in optimizing performance and self-regulation. *Journal of Experimental Social Psychology*, 53, 70–78.

4 Cohen, G. L., Aronson, J. & Steele, C. M. (2000). When beliefs yield to evidence: Reducing biased evaluation by affirming the self. *Personality and Social Psychology Bulletin*, 26, 1151–64.

5 Schmeichel, B. J. & Vohs, K. (2009). Self-affirmation and self-control: Affirming core values counters ego depletion. *Journal of Personality and Social Psychology*, 96, 770–82.

6 Schaufeli, W. B., Bakker, A. B. & Salanova, M. (2006). The measurement of work engagement with a short questionnaire. *Educational and Psychological Measurement*, 66, 701–16.

7   For just one example, see: Bakker, A. B. & Bal, P. M. (2010). Weekly work engagement and performance: A study among starting teachers. *Journal of Occupational and Organizational Psychology*, 83, 189–206.

8   Wrzesniewski, A. & Dutton, J. E. (2001). Crafting a job: Revisioning employees as active crafters of their work. *Academy of Management Review*, 26, 179–201.

9   Bakker, A. B., Tims, M. & Derks, D. (2012). Proactive personality and job performance: The role of job crafting and work engagement. *Human Relations*, 65, 1359–78.

10 Petrou, P., Demerouth, E., Peeters, M. C. W. *et al.* (2012). Crafting a job on a daily basis: Contextual correlates and the link to work engagement. *Journal of Organizational Behavior*, 33, 1120–41.

11 Berg, J. M., Wrzesniewski, A. & Dutton, J. E. (2010). Perceiving and responding to challenges in job crafting at different ranks: When proactivity requires adaptivity. *Journal of Organizational Behavior*, 31, 158–86.

12 van den Heuvel, M., Demerouti, E. & Peeters, M. (2012). Succesvol job craften door middel van een groepstraining [Succesful job crafting through group training]. In J. de Jonge, M. Peeters, S. Sjollema & H. de Zeeuw (eds.), *Scherp in werk: 5 routes naar optimale inzetbaarheid* (pp 27–49). Assen: Koninklijke van Gorcum BV.

13 Job crafting has benefited Chinese employees, for example: Lu, C.-Q., Wang, H.-J., Lu, J.-J. *et al.* (2014). Does work engagement increase person-job fit? The role of job crafting and job insecurity. *Journal of Vocational Behavior*, 84, 142–52.

14 Hornung, S., Rousseau, D. M., Weigle, M. *et al.* (2014). Redesigning work through idiosyncratic deals. *European Journal of Work and Organizational Psychology*, 23, 608–26.

Index